CORNISH ENGI G

1801 - 2001

TWO CENTURIES OF INDUSTRIAL EXCELLENCE IN CAMBORNE

BY
CLIVE CARTER
Lef an mor

First Edition 2001

CompAir

Published by CompAir UK, Camborne, Cornwall, TR14 8DS.
Printed by C A Print & Stationers Ltd., Camborne.
Front cover design Peter Savage, Penzance.

Republished Trevithick Society 2001

Acknowledgements:

Mr N.T. Holman; Mr A.F.M. Holman; Mr Jim Hodge; Mr Allen Buckley; Mr H.Blackwell; Mr K. Brown; Mr Eric Edmonds; Mr Brian Earl; Mr Gerald Williams; Mr David Thomas; Mr Milton Thomas; Mr Brian Watkins; Mrs Carol Polglase; Mrs O.P. Veal; Mr Peter Savage; Mr Peter Joseph, Tim Parr, Justin Brooke, T.B. Pinnington

Poldark Mining Company; Trevithick Society; Geevor Tin Mine Heritage Centre; Corporation of Trinity House; Trevithick Trust;

At CompAir UK:

Mr Clive Tayton Operations Director; Mr Mike Tredrea Human Resources Manager. Mr Bill Dowse, Technical Publications Department especially Mr Gary Tamblyn and Mr Nigel Willoughby.

ISBN 0 904040 53 4

Contents

Nicholas Holman

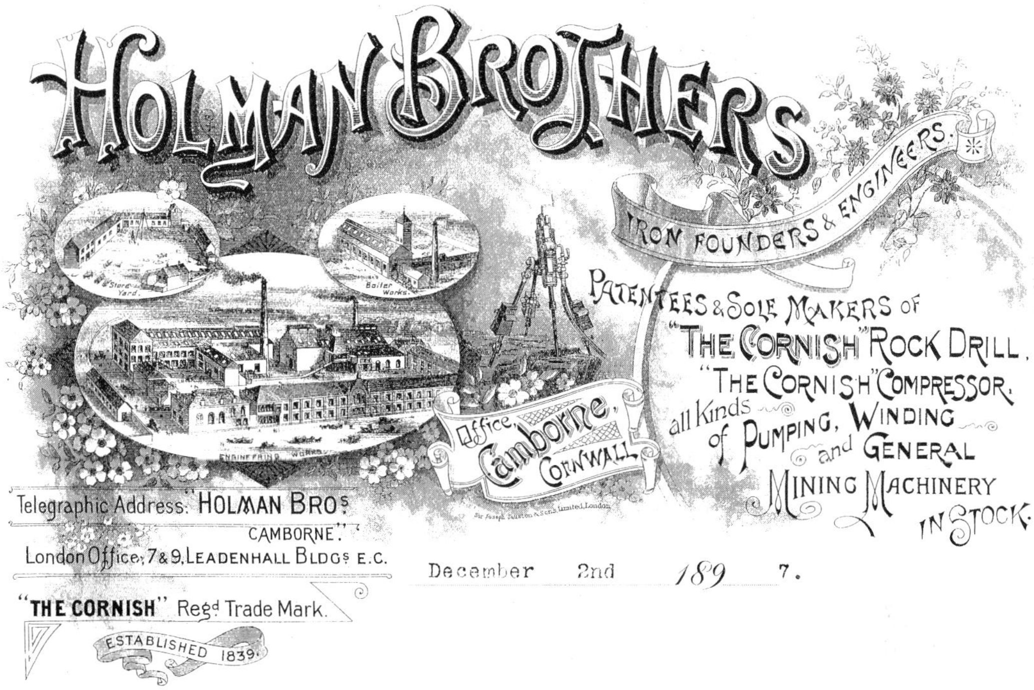

Chapter One

A Dynasty of Engineers

"In a large and lofty building, supported by pillars of iron, with great black apertures in the upper walls, open to the external air; echoing to the roof with the beating of hammers and the roar of furnaces, mingled with the hissing of red hot metal plunged into water, and a hundred strange and unearthly noises never heard elsewhere; in this gloomy place, moving like demons among the flame and smoke, dimly and fitfully seen, flushed and tormented by the burning fires, and wielding great weapons, a faulty blow from any one of which must have crushed some workman' s skull, a number of men laboured like giants.... others drew forth, with clashing, noise, upon the ground, great sheets of glowing steel, emitting insupportable heat, and a dull deep light...."

Charles Dickens
"The Old Curiosity Shop" 1841

The founder of the Holman dynasty was not, surprisingly, an engineer but a man of the soil and the plough. Nicholas Holman was born at St. Allen near Truro in 1716 and as a young man was brought to Tehidy Manor near Camborne to be a farm servant to the aristocratic Basset Family. On Boxing Day 1743 he married Anne Rowe of Camborne and they set up home on a small farm belonging to the Bassets, at Menadarva, a tiny hamlet tucked into a deep river valley sheltered from the westerly gales which drove across the bleak Atlantic cliffs of North Cornwall. The family's life must have been hard, governed by the seasons and the farming calendar, their isolation occasionally disturbed by gangs of Camborne miners heading for the cliffs to loot some wrecked ship. Each day Nicholas Holman rode to Tehidy along a rough track that ran across the moors or along the banks of the '*Red River*'. A generation earlier the river had flowed clear and fresh while trout could be caught from the ancient Menadarva bridge. Now it was coloured red by the slimes from the Camborne mines, and the scores of tin streams whose waterwheels and machinery crowded the banks.

This ever-present reminder of the money to be made from mining never tempted Nicholas

Far removed from the grime and bustle of a busy foundry John Holman and his family enjoy a game of croquet on the Lawn of Foundry House in the summer of 1880. His sons, John Henry and James Miners, dressed in the height of Victorian fashion, are already skilled engineers and directors of their father's company.

Holman, who remained a faithful retainer of the Basset family all his life. He was a capable man who later rose to become a bailiff under Lord De Dunstanville and was also remarkably enlightened, allowing each of his eight children the opportunity to follow the career of their own choice. Emanuel remained at home and ran the farm '*as long as he was able*'; Richard became a miller and Nicholas a Customsman, who later had the misfortune to be drowned at sea. John and James became copper miners, his daughter Mary married a Camborne Goldsmith and Grace was a tailoress who used to brush the plush and velvets of Lord De Dunstanville.

William Holman chose to become a mine blacksmith and through him arose what was to become two dynasties of Cornish engineers. He could not have chosen better, as these were the amazing years when the burgeoning Industrial Revolution forever changed the people and landscape of West Cornwall. This hothouse atmosphere of technological development created a breed of men whose sons and grandsons would make Cornish engineering famous from the Rocky Mountains to the Witwatersrand.

Mine smiths not merely shoed horses but were expected to make up and sharpen tools, work and rivet copper, brass and wrought iron and, increasingly, to assist the '*Viewers*'. These were travelling erectors who were setting up the first steam engines on the copper mines and demanding unheard of standards of metalworking. Methods were still crude; the Cornish engineer Robert Mitchell wrote years later that '*our blacksmiths knew nothing, comparatively speaking, of the proper method of working iron and steel, of making screw taps and plates for cutting these large adjusting screws so very useful and necessary in mining, yet so little thought on by the Cornish as by the inhabitants of the Pellow islands...*' They were soon to learn, and the skill and enterprise of Cornish engineers was to out shine that of Boulton and Watt.

In October 1772 William Holman married Mary Reed and they went to live at Pool near

In 1880 foundrymen pause in their work for the benefit of an early photographer who captured the busy Holman erection shop, which is crowded with the cast iron beds and components of two steam winders. The shop is lit by gas and well equipped with drills and lathes which are driven by belts and line shafting, worked by a small steam engine.

In 1887 John Henry Holman, standing far right wearing a bowler hat poses proudly with his men, including Mr Miller, the first company secretary, far left with a large beard, while seated on the yard at far left is the very young Ben Cock, who would spend his working life with Holmans.

Camborne, deep in the heart of the copper country. Besides general mining work he began to build boilers, very successfully despite the fact that it had taken decades to produce boilers adequate for even the low pressures of the early atmospheric engines. He soon had a large family, including Nicholas Holman who was born on the 3rd of August 1777; just five years junior to Richard Trevithick who lived just up the road and would become a close friend in later life. Nicholas spent his formative years working for his father and in 1801 when only twenty-four, he set up his own works to build boilers at Pool and rapidly established a first class reputation for workmanship. He may have made, or at least helped to assemble, the boiler for Trevithick's road locomotive, the famous '*Roaring Puffing Devil*' which made the trip up Camborne Hill on Christmas Eve that same year. He married Ann Harvey of Illogan and in 1803 Nicholas Holman Jnr. was born, one of three sons. At an early age he was taken away from Pool school to serve as yard boy and foundry messenger, often having to stand before the giant figure of Cap'n Dick himself and repeat complicated orders and receive instructions, already knowing that the engineer's kindly ways were matched by a notoriously short temper. Nicholas Senior's friendship with Trevithick brought dividends, though the great engineer's erratic business methods drove all around him to despair. In 1813 he built two of Trevithick's revolutionary Cornish boilers for a 24 inch high pressure steam pole engine which Capt. Samuel Grose was erecting on Beer Alston lead Mine on the Tamar. Trevithick as usual fumbled the '*cash flow*' and in a letter urgently requested that 'the workmen making your boilers want *an advance of cash to enable them to finish. They provide the iron and the labour for which they are to receive 42L per ton for the boiler when finished; the weight will be about 8 tons. You may send this money to Mr Sims or to me, or otherwise you might direct it to Mr N Holman, boiler maker, Pool....100L will satisfy them for the present...'* Trevithick again wrote later '*Gentlemen you have the bill for sundry expenses paid on the Beerlalston Boiler which I have advanced to the Smith, N. Holman, long since to enable them to*

The Holman foundry dominated the eastern end of Camborne for over a century, and here in about 1906, a Camborne to Redruth tramcar pauses, and there is an interested crowd gathered in front of the Centenary Chapel ('Centnery' to all good Camborne men) where the Holmans and most of the mining gentry are buried.

Nicholas Holman established his engineering reputation by building excellent boilers back in the days of Richard Trevithick, and after iron plates were replaced by rolled steel they were exported to every mining camp in the world.

finish them, would you wish a bill to be drawn on you by Holman for their balance due or shall I draw the bill on you and send you Holman's receipt? ...'

Trevithick came to Nicholas Holman for boilers for the high-pressure engines which he contracted to ship out to the Peruvian silver mines. On 22nd May 1813 he wrote '*A great part of the wrought - iron work and the boilers I have arranged in Cornwall*'. Just a few weeks later in typical whirlwind fashion, Trevithick writes again that '*Yesterday I engaged all the boiler plate in the county, which will be sent today to the different workmen. The master smiths that I have engaged are the best in the kingdom. I have obligated them to put the best quality of iron, and to be delivered at Falmouth within four months. I have been obliged to give them a greater price than I expected, otherwise they would not turn aside their usual business for a short job of four months*'. Obviously Nicholas Holman, despite his respect and friendship for Trevithick was becoming very wary of the engineers disregard for money and the latter soon made arrangements that '*boiler builders here, to weigh and pay at the end of every week*'.

The plates were not to be assembled as, like the engines and the rest of the machinery, they had to be carried up the mountain tracks of the Andes on the backs of mules, plate by plate, and riveted up on the mines. The boilers were ready by the end of September 1813 and formed part of a very large consignment, recorded in Trevithick's account book as being shipped from Penryn.

Holman's business continued to prosper and he took a contract to build boilers for Wheal Vor Mine near Helston. Young Nicholas was sent across to prepare the tools and look after the money as Thomas Jenkins, the Pool foreman, was illiterate. Soon afterwards Nicholas Snr. was

Unlike the bigger Cornish foundries, Holmans seldom made large Cornish engines but for a century they regularly cast the heavy and often complicated pit and pump work like this 'Angle Bob' ready to be despatched from No.1 works complete with balance box and a truly splendid brass makers plate.

approached by Robert Mitchell, one of the proprietors of the new Copperhouse Foundry at Hayle, a ready rival to the Harvey Foundry just down river. He was offered the job of manager of the boiler works but, now middle-aged, he was not inclined to leave his home and business at Pool. Instead he suggested that young Nicholas, subject to his father's help, took the position. Nicholas Snr. thoroughly trusted his son and rarely visited Copperhouse and when he did, he '*took up his portion with clean hands never having been called upon to do a days work*'.

When Nicholas Jnr. left Copperhouse to set up his own foundry at St. Just in 1834, he '*recommended my brother William as a proper person to succeed me and offered myself to render him assistance at any time if required, which was agreed to*'. William was then only twenty-one but such was the training he received at their father's works, he was readily taken on at Copperhouse.

James Holman, the youngest brother, born in 1825, would eventually manage the Pool works for his father and would be the only one to remain a bachelor. John Holman, the middle son, born in 1819 was scarcely twenty when, doubtless enthused by his brothers success at St. Just, he

The moulding shop at No.1 at the turn of the century, a scene that hardly changed for a century, until the advent of modern techniques in the 1960s

decided to set up his own business. In 1839 he established a small boiler works and foundry at Camborne and this eastern end of the town would for the next one hundred and fifty years become in effect '*Fort Holman*', with all the noise, bustle and smell emitted by a busy foundry.

Camborne had changed considerably since the days of Trevithick. From a few houses lining a muddy street around the church it had grown into a busy small town that would soon be on the new railway line up from Hayle to Redruth. Indeed, John Holman's foundry was built beside the magnificent Wesleyan Chapel that gave its name to the new street. He was a very shrewd and excellent businessman, whose success paralleled that of his brother's foundry at St. Just, where the legend '*if its metal take it to Holmans*' might easily have been coined for both small foundries. Unlike his brother, he was far better at mining speculation and invested in most of the Camborne mines, he enjoying the privilege, like many other entrepreneurs, that as both supplier and shareholder he rarely lost money.

He continued the family speciality of building the iron plate boilers which generated the high-pressure steam needed by the pumping engines of the 100 mines between Carn Brea and Lands End. Yet neither he nor Nicholas saw themselves as rivals to the three great Cornish foundries of Perran, Harvey and Copperhouse, where the engineering heirs of Woolf and Trevithick brought the Cornish high-pressure steam engine to perfection and worldwide use. In contrast, although they were both heavily involved in making boilers and mining machinery, the Holmans relied upon a steady and well-founded, if unspectacular trade which embraced a vast variety of other customers. John Holman made agricultural implements like his cousin, who had built the first iron plough in West Cornwall at his new wharf-side Foundry in 1841, as an advert in the West Briton of 1846 demonstrates.

'*John Holman. Boiler Builder and Farming Implements manufacturers, Camborne, begs most respectfully to call the attention of his friends and agriculturists generally, to his improved portable and other Potato and Turnip steaming apparatus, which for cheapness, utility, and economy he is confident cannot be excelled*'.

Old Nicholas Holman died in August 1862, leaving the Pool Works to his brother James, but by then John Holman's own foundry was well established. His first son, James Henry, was born in 1853 and the second, James Miners, in 1857. Both were destined to make the name 'Holman Brothers' famous in every mining camp in the world. They duly did their apprenticeships; James doing his at Camborne but John went to the famous Birmingham '*Cornwall*' Works of the expatriate family of Cornish engineers, the Tangye family. George Tangye, one of the partners, actually did his own apprenticeship at Holman's before he and his brother James migrated to the Midlands to establish their own engineering empire.

The Holman machine shop around 1890

By the time the Holman boys finished their apprenticeships, the fabled Cornish '*Copper Kingdom*' was fast sinking into ruin as the copper mines, already forced to sink deeper in pursuit of their waning mineral riches, were rivalled by vast copper strikes in Australia and on the Great Lakes of North America. To worsen matters, the price of tin began the often-violent fluctuations which almost destroyed Cornish mining by the turn of the century. Depression and slump made inevitable the fate of the big Cornish foundries, whose fortunes were far too closely wedded to those of the ailing copper mines. There were the first warnings that the era of the great 'Cornish' pumping engine was ending, as these once innovative and technological wonders were left bobbing in the wake of the ship of progress, which would increasingly rely on oil, electricity and compressed air. Perran and Copperhouse Foundries had both gone by the early 1870s, while Harvey of Hayle embarked on shipbuilding to fill the gaps in their order books, but the glory days of their massive foundry were almost over.

John Holman remained as versatile and resilient as ever and was easily able to survive these hard times and his price list for 1880 demonstrates; the 'Camborne Foundry & Engine Works' could produce engine cylinders and beams, stamp gearing and flywheels, stamp heads, wagons, kibbles, skips, and picks and shovels; while *'Plain Cylindrical Boilers, made of the Best Plates and Best Rivet iron' were 18/- per cwt'.*

To transport their foundry material and other goods, John Holman bought a traction engine, which in January 1885 hauled 13 tons of tin concentrate to the smelter at Point, near Devoran. This was the first load to arrive behind a traction engine, and the trip was accomplished despite heavy frost on Brea Hill and around Tuckingmill. Often the engine was sent down to their Holman cousins at St. Just for boiler repairs. John Holman, who always prefaced his letters to Camborne '*Dear Cousins*', unashamedly used his influence as a shareholder in the St. Just mines to win contracts for them as in January 1887 when he wrote regarding a big job for Botallack, hoping that '*the Lion's share of it will come to our beloved cousins in Camborne*'

John Holman never built the really big Cornish engines, though in 1897 a 28-inch engine was built for Dolcoath stamps. Usually he supplied small handy engines that attracted a wide variety of customers from Tehidy Saw Mills to Trevarno tinstreams. John Mills, a Camborne builder, praised his Holman engine which '*drove a 30 inch saw with perfect ease and the amount of work that can be done with proper appliances is astounding*'. *Even Michael Loam wrote that the 'little horizontal engine you sent us this summer is working exceedingly well.. and shall be happy to recommend it*'.

A tattered notebook provides an insight into the everyday work of the foundry;

21st Dec. Make one Bevel Wheel East Pool Pulveriser at 4 days at 1/6- Commenced Monday 1/2 day'.

W. F. J. Harvey make core boxes and sweep for centre piece Dolcoath Stamps. Also alter arm. 1/2 day'.

9th Nov. John Veal had 6 days to make 3 foot 6 Slab with lining best brass work etc. for Capt. Rabling

W H Carbis make 12 Bell mouth kibbles at 6 days 2/6- Carbis 1/6- Boy. commenced Friday 10 am. Gained 2/6-. boy 1/6-. 1/2 day.

N Curry make 12" Roll 3" wide. Time 4 1/2 days. Commenced 1 Aug. 1 30 pm.'

This was the legendary Nicholas Curry, '*Mr Nicky*'. Born at Gwinear, he joined Holmans at the age of eighteen in 1888 and rose from a humble fitter to become works manager, eventually retiring after fifty-eight years service.

In 1870 the Holman sons, despite their relatively young age, had joined John as directors of their company. They were completely complementary to each other; John Henry, brilliant and innovative engineer and James Miners, a very shrewd and astute businessman. Together they laid the foundations of what would become a worldwide company and the tool of their success was the rock drill, or '*boring machine*' as it was then popularly known.

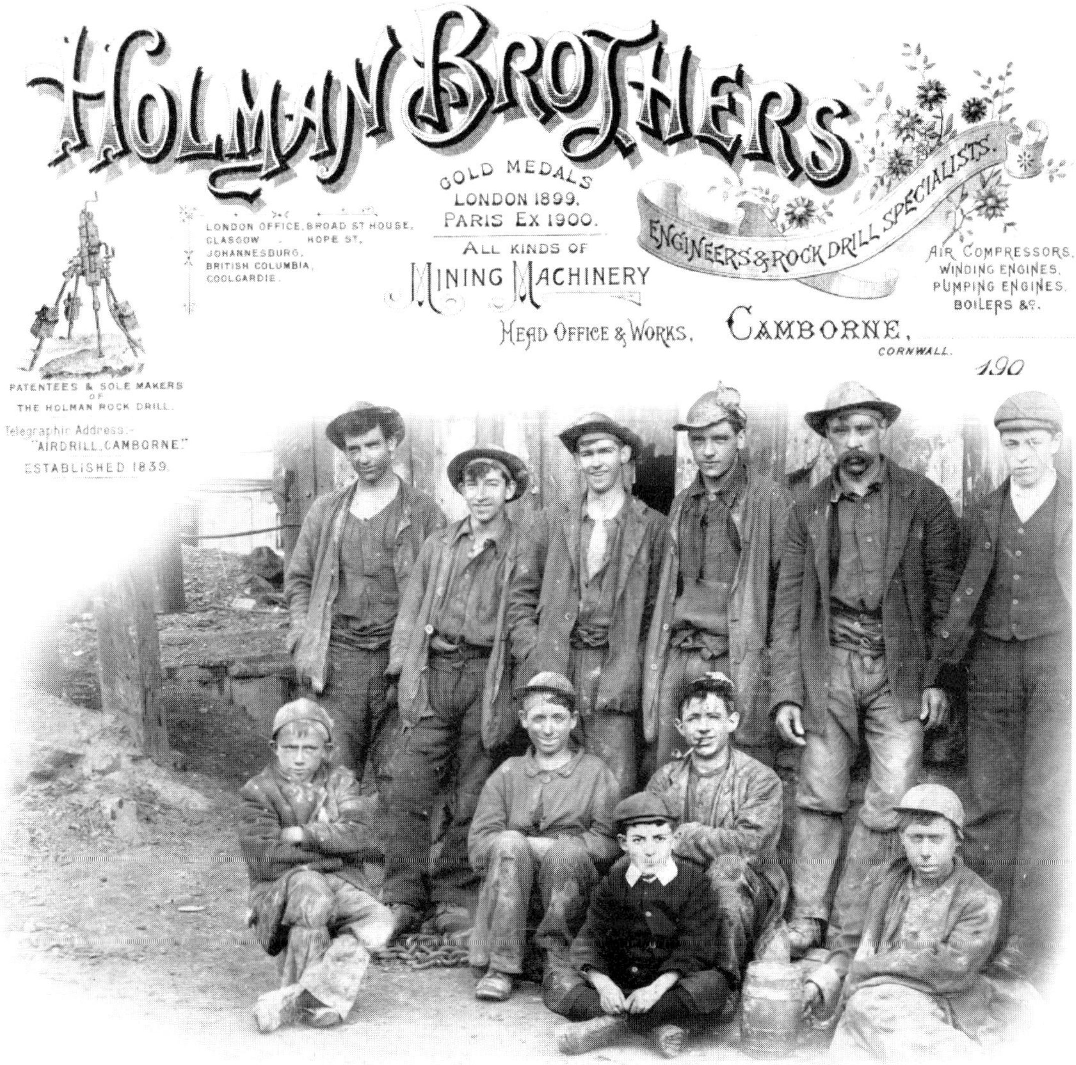

Chapter Two

The 'Cornish' Rock Drill

The true percussive rock drill was essentially an American invention, born of the vital need to break a technological impasse that threatened the great designs to span that continent. Railroad Engineers and contractors had to pierce hills and mountains on a scale and speed never before envisaged and could not afford to drive their tunnels by '*Hand Labour*'. In the words of the famous American ballad, '*John Henry*' might have been determined '*not to let that steam drill take my place*', and to '*die with a hammer in my hand*', but the laborious method of drilling by hand to tunnel through solid rock was about to be revolutionised.

Fifty years before, Richard Trevithick had invented a rail-mounted steam rotary borer which helped quarry large blocks of limestone for the Plymouth Breakwater. In 1838, the American Singer brothers had built a machine where the drill was raised by a steam piston and allowed to drop by gravity, boring what was known in Cornwall as '*a downer*'. Singer drills were used on the Illinois and Michigan Canal

Until the arrival of machine drilling, any advance through the solid rock relied upon 'Hand labour', or 'Beating the Boryer' as it was known in Cornish mines. Here miners working 'Double handed' demonstrate their skills in Cook's Kitchen around 1893, a scene that would have been familiar to the Roman miners of Rio Tinto and a technique which inspired Richard Trevithick to build the first rotary rock drill eighty years before.

and in enlarging the Erie Canal. Although the brothers never pursued their ideas, Isaac went on to perfect the sewing machine.

The real ancestor of the modern rock drill was the '*Lance*', patented on 27 March 1849 by John Couch, surely a Cornish expatriate, of Philadelphia. His steam driven machine drill used a heavy flywheel, ratchet and a piston to create a momentum which drove the drill '*lance like*' against the rock face at any angle. Two years later J. J. Fowle, his principal assistant, took the design a stage further and became the first engineer to propel the drill against the rock by the direct action of steam upon a piston, a motion that was a universal feature of rock drills for the next fifty years. He also used a ratchet and pawl to rotate the drill steel and replaced the '*Lance*' motion by setting the drill on a cross head, making it far steadier.

Fowle's basic designs were developed by other engineers like Charles Burleigh who, having bought Fowle's patent, coupled the drill steel directly to the piston, another feature that was to be a standard feature of rock drills for decades. Forty of his big steam drills were used to drive the Hoosac Railroad Tunnel under the hills of western Massachusetts by General Herman Haupt, a veteran US Army Engineer, who had built roads through the wilderness and had been promoted for services to the Union after the Battle of Bull Run. His own powerful rock drills were also used to drive the Hoosac but he preferred compressed air to steam, and the appalling underground conditions were then so radically improved '*that everybody was convinced that air was preferable and no more talk of steam was heard*'. Burleigh patents were in turn acquired by the Ingersoll brothers, whose company merged with that of the innovative Harry Sergeant in 1884 to form the famous Ingersoll Sergeant rock drill company.

A greater epic than the Hoosac was the driving of the eight-mile tunnel to take the railway from Paris to Turin under the 12,000 ft. Mont Cenis in the Italian Alps. Work began in 1857 and hand labour and gunpowder blasting produced a weekly advance and casualty rate reminiscent of a bad spell in the siege lines outside Sevastopol. Germain Someiller, the engineer commanding the French heading at Fourneaux in Savoy, produced his own large machine drill, with air being supplied by compressors of his own design, driven by large waterwheels. There were many setbacks and the work was very slow by modern standards, but the Mont Cenis Tunnel was finally driven through on Christmas Day 1870 by Borer No 45, a massive multi- drill rig mounted on a

In 1868 Frederick Doering, a German mining engineer from the Rhur, brought the first rock drill to Cornwall and, though tested in Tincroft and Dolcoath mine, proved too fragile and complicated to survive working in the Camborne mines.

railway bogie and towing its own water tank to de-sludge the holes.

All this innovation and expertise was displayed to great acclaim at the Paris Exhibition of 1867 and created extraordinary interest among the more forward thinking Cornish mining men. To many, this sudden outburst of mechanisation was the answer to the desperate state of Cornish mining. '*Cousin Jack*' was going to suffer the same fate as '*John Henry*'. Later that same year, many of those who exhibited at Paris came to Cornwall with their machines, including General Haupt. The Cornishmen seemed to have been mildly bewildered by the plethora of machine drills offered to them by a variety of entrepreneurs, all eager to test their machines in such a prestigious mining country. Many more conservative Cornish mining men opposed mechanisation, but in 1868 Captain William Teague, a legend in Cornish mining, invited Frederick Doering of Rhurort in the Rhur to test his machine at Tincroft Mine. Despite initial and spectacular success the 'Doering' drill was a failure, not only there but also at Dolcoath, where the formidable Captain Josiah Thomas had arranged a trial for the German machine.

Many mining men became convinced that a special drill was needed for the Cornish mines and their quest for such a machine brought many drill companies down to the Cornish mining country, especially when another slump in tin made mechanisation even more urgent. Capt. Josiah Thomas, a staunch champion of the rock drill, chose the 'Barrow', developed by James Hosking, '*a smith we sent to Barrow about twenty years since*' and Harold Blackwell, an engine smith who also worked at the Park Iron Pit, near Barrow-in-Furness. With a heavy cast gunmetal body the 'Barrow', which was cranked forward along the cradle by the same handle that rotated the drill steel, began driving the 314 level west in Old Sump Shaft in October 1875. The drill had to

Hand drilling competitions were always highly popular at Cornish festivals and galas, right up to the last days of Geevor Mine in the 1980's. The 'Cousin Jacks' took the tradition with them to the foreign mining camps but in reality drilling a 'Downer' on a summers afternoon , cheered on by an enthusiastic crowd bore little resemblance to the same job done in the depths of Dolcoath or Cook's Kitchen.'

be redesigned after receiving a fearsome pounding, boring rock so hard '*it would scratch like glass*'. Yet the 'Barrow' crew drove four times faster than the Hand Labour team driving a level 12 fathoms above their heads. Captain Thomas was delighted and bitterly criticised the die-hards who opposed the rock drill, likening them to those who preferred to cross the Atlantic in a sailing ship while he preferred sailing on '*a Cunarder*'. He even allowed Leila Noble of Rome Georgia, granddaughter of a Cornish emigrant, to inspect the 'Barrow' at the bottom of New Sump Shaft when she went underground down the man engine and 30 fathoms of ladder roads at Dolcoath in June 1879.

More rock drills were offered to the Cornishmen who must have keenly read their makers superlative adverts in the 'Morning Journal', or the letters that reflected the bitter rivalry between the companies themselves. The American 'MacKean', a development of the General Haupt tunnelling drill, was put to work at South Roskear and another American drill, the Burleigh, in Rocks and Goonbarrow Mine. Carn Brea chose the enormously powerful rock drills of the celebrated Major Beaumont R.E., of the Diamond Rock Boring Co. who specialised in tunnelling and deep boring. The cost was appalling and the Beaumont's were really not suitable for Cornish mines.Its only distinction was to be the first machine to be responsible for a fatal rock drill accident when a miner drilled into a miss- fired shot in Sept. 1879. Capt. Thomas had already contracted with another rock drill company, Ulathorne & Co., to use their 'Champion' drill, and firmly believed '.. *the time is not far distant when people will not think of working Cornish mines without boring machines* '.

This technological revolution was not lost on the Holman boys, but how they became converts to machine drilling is a matter of conjecture. They were both astute Cornishmen who realised that mechanisation and mining were inseparable, and that the future meant radical change, if they were not to share the fate of the big foundries. Their Camborne works was far less vulnerable but the demand for mining machinery in Cornwall itself was shrinking and the Holman boys became convinced that compressed air, rather than steam, was the key to a worldwide market. They already made very successful air compressors and it must have seemed quite logical to make rock drills as well. Such was their enthusiasm that their father got so heartily tired of their talk of rock drills that he forbade them to speak of them over the breakfast table.

One of the better early rock drills was the 'Barrow', which was built under licence by the Cornish engineer Michael Loam at his foundry in Saltash, and seen here at work in Dolcoath in 1875.

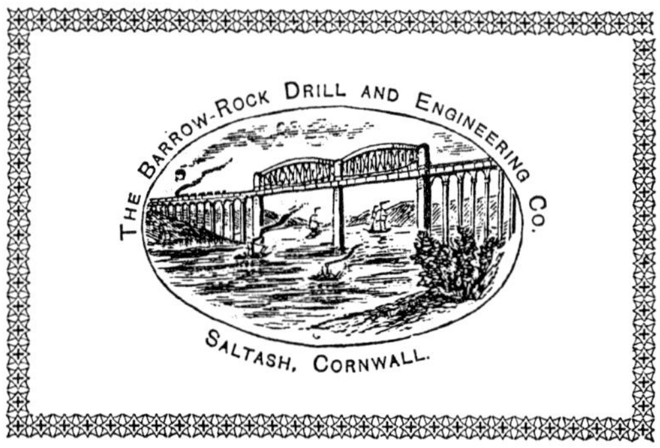

John Holman retired in 1880 and the boys took over the Camborne works and immediately began experimenting with rock drills. Already in Cornwall was James McCulloch, an English- born Scottish mining engineer, who around 1870 had worked for the 'Burleigh' Rock drill company. He had also spent several years as a contractor driving levels at the Rio Tinto in Spain. Abrasive and self - opinionated, McCulloch's expertise with rock drills was undeniable and he designed several machines and tunnelling carriages. He had recently arrived as an agent for Hathorn & Co., whose very successful 'Eclipse' rock drills had won

A Silver Medal by drilling four times the speed of hand labour at a contest held at Falmouth Docks in August 1879. The Cornishmen had reservations, fearing the drills' valves were too sensitive and they also had their pet hate, automatic feed. Yet within a few months the 'Eclipse' had captured East Pool mine, second only to Dolcoath, driving the 180 west to uncover a huge run of tin ground. The 'Eclipse' even penetrated the notoriously conservative mining country around St. Just, when the adventurers chose it to drive northwards into Wheal Cock, which was being developed after the abandonment of the famous Crowns section.

How Mr Culloch met the Holman boys is unknown. The 'Eclipse' agents were often at Dolcoath where John Holman was a shareholder; in May 1879 he was arguing with Captain Thomas regarding the cost of replacing the underground tram iron rails with steel. There was also a big meeting at '*Abraham's Hotel*' at Camborne, which was attended by all the mine captains and engineers including Captain Henderson of the 'Eclipse'.

McCulloch may have already abandoned the 'Eclipse' and joined the Holmans, as in October 1880 they filed a patent for an '*Improved machine for drilling rocks* '. Building the prototype was no easy task as, although the Holman foundry was well equipped, a rock drill required new jigs and tooling, and the tolerances required for compressed air were finer than for steam pressure. There were patent drawings but the standard procedure was to make the part first, then the drawing and the pattern.

In April 1881 the Holmans signed their first agreement with James McCulloch. The witness, interestingly, was the first works manager, Alfred Harvey, who had been apprenticed to their father in 1847 at twelve years of age and three years later had begun his foundry career in the smiths shop. The agreement stated that, once manufacturing costs were deducted, the actual selling price would be then mutually determined and the profits would be shared equally. The Holmans would advance sufficient money to McCulloch to secure the patent on his tool holder and also finance other developments, but the cost of marketing and publicity would be shared equally. The new 'Cornish Rock Drill' made its debut at a rock drill contest held at Dolcoath Mine by the Mining Institute of Cornwall on 8th Dec. 1881. Drilling against the McCulloch's old partners, 'Eclipse', and a 'Barrow' brought up from underground, the '*Cornish made a winning debut, and 'by greater durability and special adaptability to be more suitable for the mines of the West than those now in use, a point which experience, of course, can alone satisfactorily decide*'.

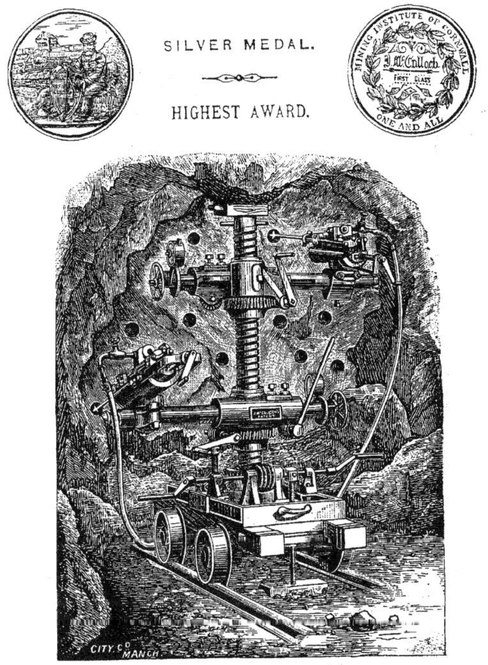

Mc.CULLOCH'S PATENT HEADING CAR.

Captain Teague, undaunted by his experience with the Beaumont drill, immediately ordered 'Cornish' rock drills for Carn Brea where four of them speedily drove 7 fathoms in a month. This inspired his son William Teague Jnr. to work on his own drill, the 'Cornish Boy', which was used with his patent ventilator in several mines.

The success of the 'Cornish' Rock Drill led to another agreement between McCulloch and the Holmans, which allowed them the costs for developing the prototypes of the 3 in and $3\,^{1}/_{4}$ inch drills and another £84 towards maintaining the drills which Capt. Teague put into Carn Brea. Yet there was the first intimation that the partnership was in trouble; clause 6 stated '*That as soon as Holman Bros. receive payment of any account arising out of the sale of a Drills.... they shall pay*

James McCulloch half of his half share until such time that he has paid back the money advanced on his behalf for Patenting Advertisements, Printing etc. when he shall receive the whole of his share'.
A year later another rock drill contest was hosted by the Royal Cornwall Polytechnic Society when they had to bore into a large granite boulder supplied by Freeman & Sons of Penryn and a very hard tin stone, full of '*Vugs*' from Dolcoath Mine. The 'Cornish' drill went up against not only its old rivals, the 'Eclipse', the 'Excelsior', the 'Barrow' and the 'Beaumont' but also a new machine, made by W. S. Stephens of the South Crofty Iron Works, alias the '*Rock Drill Hospital*', or as it was better known in later years, the 'Climax' Rock Drill Company. The two-day trial was dogged by poorly tempered drills and machine breakdowns; Captain Josiah Thomas considered it was more of a test of drill steels than the drills.

Nobody was satisfied and soon old rivalries reached the letter columns of the 'Mining Journal'. Enraged by the claims of an '*Occasional Correspondent*' who thought the "Eclipse' superior to all other drills, James McCulloch defended the performance and quality of the '*Cornish*' Rock Drill. The two feed screws driven by a central cog wheel ensured the machine stayed in balance on the cradle without wear or jamming and the machine used half the amount of air consumed by the 'Eclipse'. He roundly attacked his old partners, claiming that Hathorn & Co. were so worried by the new competition that they consequently '*fall back on the pen to what they fail to accomplish by fair contest*'.

Hathorn angrily rebuffed McCulloch, claiming that he imagined that '*by maligning the 'Eclipse' drill, he can enhance the value of the Cornish drill but we think differently.' and that 'it was us, Hathorn & Co. who first introduced - Mr McCulloch into Cornwall and found him the machinery to take his first contract*'. They ended by likening him to the exhausted snake which, on being taken home by a man, then bit its benefactor.

'*Occasional Correspondent*' returned to the fray claiming that the 'Cornish' rock drill was over-engineered, over-manned, and that on the day before the contest it had broken down at East Pool and been replaced by an 'Eclipse'. The Holman boys joined the argument over the contest and defended their drills in East Pool, saying just one machine had been out of action for only a couple of hours. The 'Cornish' drill which Capt. Teague had used underground in Tincroft for the last nine months without ever having been back to the fitting shop. This was the same machine which beat the 'Eclipse' in the trial in December 1881, and anyway the 'Eclipse' drills tested recently in Dolcoath used so much air that it was known as the '*Consumptive Valve Drill*'. Michael Loam, the resident engineer at Dolcoath who was building the 'Barrow' drill under licence, joined the fray when he sent out with a sales leaflet, a distorted copy of a letter by Frederick Doering about his drills' performance at Rio Tinto. The McKean Company, who were driving the St.Gothard Tunnel, then offered to take on all comers and the 'Excelsior' drill makers and the Holman boys accepted. James McCulloch continued to stoke up the general resentment but in the end there was no contest.

There was also increasing friction between him and the Holman boys, unsurprising as they belonged to the Camborne mining and engineering fraternity, notorious since the days when Boulton & Watt desperately tried to get

Closely hemmed about by pumpwork and the shaft walls, a 'Machine crew' putting down the sump of Cook's Kitchen Shaft in 1893, using a big drifter mounted on a stretcher bar. Helmets and shirts have been discarded in the intense heat as, perched on a narrow ledge they work saturated with sweat and splashed with muddy water, while the noise from the early drills was tremendous in such confined spaces.

royalties for their new engines. A breach was inevitable when McCulloch continued to object to the high cost of advertising. He insisted that they had agreed adverts would be confined only to the pages of the 'Mining Journal' and besides, when these did appear, Holmans' general mining machinery was much more prominent than the 'Cornish' Rockdrill. He also took umbrage at the way Holmans took rock drills to contests and exhibitions without consultation and then sent him the bill for half the costs.

James McCulloch returned to Huleva and Rio Tinto but was outraged by the accounts that the Holmans sent him, suspecting that though the brothers were not actually dishonest, they were offering discounts and doing deals with their friends in the mining world. Finally certain '*that all these irregularities go to show the loose system and vexilating methods Holman Brothers have*' he decided to sue them and they promptly counter claimed for £100 17s 5d. The acrimonious dispute was not settled until 13 August 1887 when they agreed to cancel all debts and each could develop the patent for the 'Cornish' Rock Drill, free from interference of the other. Holmans were still not taking chances with McCulloch and had soon secured their own rockdrill patent to cover the Spanish mines.

This era of frantic and often bitter rivalry between the rock drill companies gradually ebbed away as technical development evened out the markets. There was a final flurry in the pages of the 'Mining Journal' following an exhibition of mining held at the Crystal Palace in May 1890. James McCulloch had the largest display of all and his less than honest claims that the 'Cornish' rock drill was merely a crude prototype, whose imperfections enabled him to perfect his magnificent new 'Rio Tinto' rock drill, must have outraged the Holman boys. They were also assailed by 'Climax' who disputed Holman claims as to the merits of their valves, durability of machines and especially that they had invented the steel liners which took the wear on the cradle as the drill was wound back and forth. 'Climax' claimed to have done this years before but had strangely not patented the improvement. They made the inevitable challenge to a contest at £400 aside to split between the Miner's Hospital and a London Charity. The Holman boys, although successful in such contests, remained dubious about them and told Herbert

Thomas of the 'Cornishman' newspaper that they believed that in a trial '*lasting only a few minutes, a drill may be dismissed as worthless on account of a borer happening to be too hard or too soft although there may be no inherent defect in the drill'*, and anyway '*We prefer to stay at home and execute orders*'.

They withdrew from the argument when their father John died suddenly at the age of seventy-two while attending a missionary meeting at Camborne Wesley on 6 November 1890. He was really the last link to the early days of steam engineering and the great copper mining era, who heard tales of the great Trevithick from his own father. On the day of his funeral the Dolcoath adventurers closed their meeting so they could join other mining men and Holmans' men in a long procession through the Trelowarren where the business closed as a mark of respect.

Group of foundry workers outside the works around 1899

Foundry men finishing off a double drum winch around 1900

A splendid Camborne Group, including James Miners Holman and John Henry Holman, at the Wedding of a son of Captain Josiah Thomas, of Dolcoath Mine, who is the imposing bearded figure to the right of the Bride.

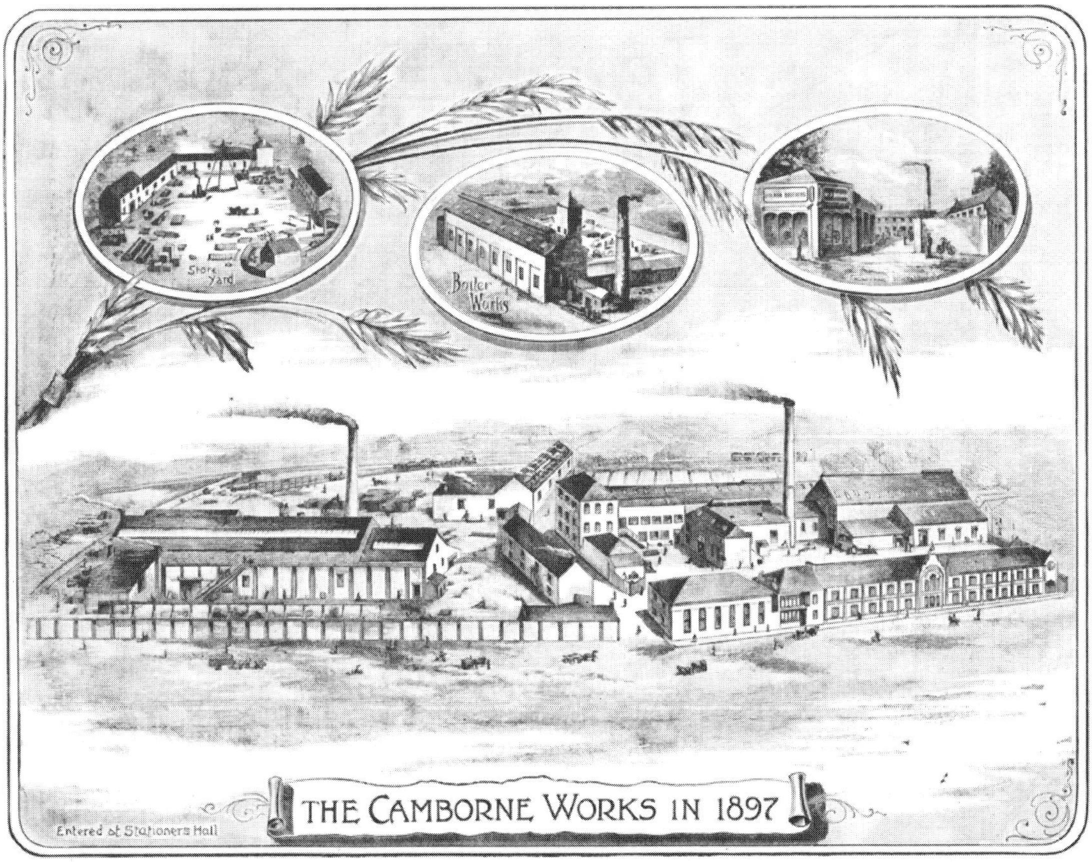

Chapter Three

" *Success to the compressor*"

(Major White of Levant Mines)

John Holman had lived long enough to see his sons create a thriving engineering works and foundry. In January 1887 they erected a big new air compressor for Dolcoath and later that same year the last ever Cornish beam whim at East Pool. Known as North Whim or more often as 'Mitchell's Whim' after its designer, the Cornish engineer F. W. Mitchell, the 30 inch cylinder engine worked at 25 SPM and could haul skips at 1000 feet per minute. At the same time they built a 16" engine with condenser and pitwork 'with a thoroughly good whistle, to be heard 2 miles off' for Mr Strauss. There were also plenty of foreign orders:-

Dec. 30, 1884 - One 3 " and one 31/2 " drills and stretcher bar. 24 bits, 1 spare valve tappet and pin for each, and clamp. For Spain.

June 18, 1885 - Two 3 " rock drills, Governor and spanners. Stretcher Bar and clamp, with hose, borers and spare parts ("duplicates") For New Zealand.

June 20, 1885 - Steam Winch. One 3 " Drill. One 3 1/2" drill. One Stretcher bar. For Australia.
25 October 1886 - Four 3 1/2" drill, 2 handles, 2 sets spanners, 4 clamps, 2 Governor cock, Pistons as per tracing For Spain

An old foundry day book tells of the work that went to fulfil these orders;

' 9 July 1888 Fitting shop. Ben Cock, Bond, G Hosking and T Penhall. To make 2 - 3 1/2 drills. Thirteen days.'

13 August 1888. Ben Cock and Bond to do all the turning including twist bars of 2 - 3 1/2 drills commenced at noon.'

' 22 Feb.1889. H Harvey and Jackson to make ,try and paint one 4 " winch. 14 days. Cylinder bored. Covers turned.'
'Ben Cock, J Hosking, T Penhall and F Miller to make four 2 1/2 drills.

13 August 1888 Ben Cock and Bond to do all the turning including twist bars of 2 3 1/2 drills. Commenced at noon.'

Eighteen year old Ben Cock was one of one of five talented brothers of an old mining family whose father was known as the *'Solomon of Tuckingmill'*. Ben's brother William 'artist, draughtsman, author and one time preacher' had, like Ben, joined Holmans in 1878 and was responsible for the magnificent artwork for the company publicity for over fifty years. Their nephew was Garstain Cox, who matured into a superb artist who would produce paintings for the famous Holman calendars. Ben Cock was a dedicated young man, eager to improve himself by study and hard work. His subsequent career was inseparable from the development of the rock drill, he rose to become works manager at No.1.

The Holmans had already set up their own small rock drilling company to carry out driving and sinking contracts for the Camborne mines. They drove at Wheal Seton where the venerable Captain Charles Thomas - father of Captain Josiah of Dolcoath - on his first visit to the mine for thirty years, was deeply impressed by the Holman machines.

The Holmans also executed what was regarded as an amazing feat of machine drilling in a Cornish mine. During the summer of 1889 Captain Bishop had brought back rock drills to Wheal Grenville after the miners objections had led to the pulling out of three 'Champions' some years

Ben Cock, began his working life at Holmans during the robust pioneering days of the early rock drills and he would serve with the company for the rest of his life, rising from a humble fitter to become works manager.

before. He also chose to improve haulage and winding at the old East Grenville engine shaft by simultaneously sinking and rising and Holmans took the contract to put up the 51-fathom raise at £31.50p a fathom. *'Raising'* was probably the least favourite underground work of all, with the drills boring almost vertically upwards above the heads of the miners, who faced a continual cascade of dust, dirt and muddy water, perched as they were on a box staging which was accessible only by ladders that disappeared into the gloom

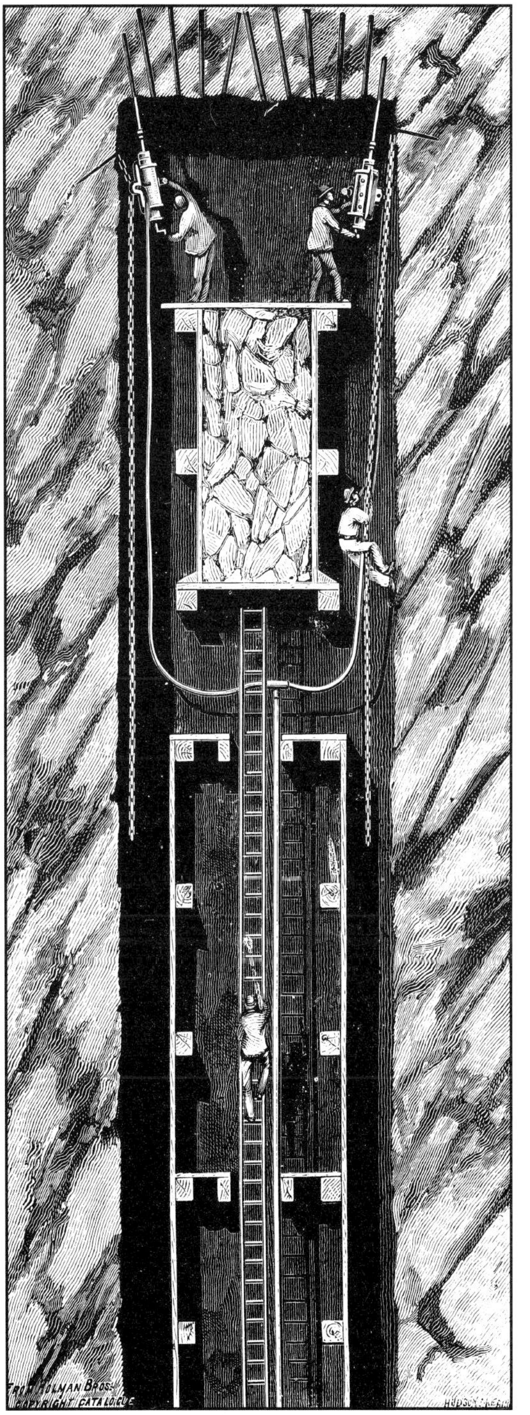

'The Grenville Rise' graphically illustrated in the Holman catalogue of 1901.

beneath their boots. There was also the pounding roar of these early drills which, also weighing over 300 lb., had to be dismounted once a round was drilled and manhandled out of the way of the blasting.

Far above the Holman crew's heads, the hand labour men were sinking the bottom of the shaft until in October 1890 they broke through. The engine shaft had been risen 300 fathoms by the Holman crew, and such was the accuracy that it was perfect on the SW corners and only a matter of inches on the NE. The Holman boys' delight was somewhat marred when an expatriate Cornish mine captain, W.J.Paul of Charter Towers, the big Queensland Gold mine, having noted the controversy between Holmans and Climax, wrote a scathing letter regarding the Grenville rise. Holmans might rise at 21 foot a month but at Charter Towers, with four Ingersoll drills they put a shaft down 50 foot in a fortnight. The Holmans ignored the potential controversy but James McCulloch, back at Huelva, quixotically rose to their defence, or rather to that of the drill he helped design in the pages of the 'Mining Journal'.

Meanwhile the Holman works continued to expand and their business largely escaped the effects of the catastrophic tin slump which almost wiped Cornwall off the World's mining map in 1896. The 'Mining World' noted during a visit in 1894 that *'the major part of what is produced is despatched to foreign mining fields... seven eighths of the work turned out here is on order for all quarters of the globe. Some of the workmen were engaged in moulding a girder-type bed for an 18 inch by 36 inch two stage air compressor....There is on view Holman's improved pumping and winding engine for steam or compressed air.. the fitting shop is one of the largest in the West of England - 200 feet by 40 feet wide. Here were found some thirty men employed on overtime making Cornish rock drills for delivery in various parts of the world'*.

Another big compressor had been built when the old committee at Carn Brea, soon to amalgamate with neighbouring Tincroft, realised that their old compressor was burning 10 tons of coal a week merely to work two 'Cornish' rockdrills sinking Old Sump Shaft. This was 3 tons more than the Tincroft air compressor needed to work double the number of drills and two Holman air winches. The Holman boys responded with a technological monster that marked the real beginning of their long tradition of building air compressors.

The first company secretary Mr Frederick Miller surrounded by his staff, including seated on the right Nicholas Curry, 'Mr Nicky', who remained with the company for sixty years.

Installed in the spring of 1894, it was a cross compound compressor with an HP cylinder 18 ins by 72 ins and an LP cylinder 34 ins by 72 ins driving an air cylinder 26 ins by 72 ins., while the flywheel alone was 15 ft in dia and weighed 14 tons. Capable of driving fifteen Holman drills and three 6 ins combined pumping and winding engines, it was 75 % more efficient and burned $1^1/_2$ tons of coal less per day than the old machine.

There was a spectacular tribute to Holman workmanship when, on a fine night in May 1904, P.C. Meneer and Engineer Rodda found the compressor house engulfed in flames with the roof about to collapse. To everybody's amazement, including Nicholas Trestrail and Capt. Penhaul, the blaze had been so swift that, apart from broken steam gauges and slightly scorched paintwork, the compressor was unharmed. Luckily the fire brigade had not been called as cold water turned on the hot iron work would have been disastrous for the engine, which was not insured. However, months later the air cylinder was found to be cracked which stopped worked for some days.

The great Dolcoath was also modernising, though the ailing Captain Josiah had largely handed over management to his son R. Arthur Thomas. Arthur already had wide experience of mining, having been manager at City & Suburban goldmine in the Transvaal for some time. His enthusiasm for mechanisation exceeded that of his father's for the *'Boring machine'* and the mine was to undergo radical transformation above and below *'Grass'*. Unsurprisingly, Holmans would do much of the work as they were both excellent engineers and large shareholders. John Henry Holman sat on the board of the Ltd company formed on 2nd October 1895. A few weeks later Michael Henry Williams, the chairman of Docloath cut the first sod of the new William's Shaft, which, once sunk 3000 feet beneath Carn Entral would supposedly modernise the entire mine. Buffeted by a sudden snow storm, the assembled company retreated down the hill to the Count House, and what an amazing assemblage they were, redolent of the wealth and power that controlled the *'Black Country'* of Cornwall. Among them were the Holman boys, Captain Josiah and three of his sons and Oliver Wethered, who would later create Geevor Tin mine. Also there were Arthur Strauss, tin broker and Liberal M.P. for the Mining Division; Frank Harvey of Harveys of Hayle and David W Bain, Mine adventurer and owner of a fleet of steam colliers. Another attendee was Major Frank Oats of St. Just, a director of De Beers and friend of Cecil Rhodes. He was a member of the Cape Parliament and had returned home to invest his wealth in Cornish mines. George H. Batten, barrister and director of the Hyderabad Deccan gold mines which had just bought a large air compressor from the Holmans, was there.

James Miners Holman himself proposed the toast *'The Neighbouring Mines'*, remarking that he hoped they would follow the example of Dolcoath which *'had broken away from the old lines and started on a new foundation'*. He was sure that young Arthur Basset of Tehidy would be equally as generous to them in off-setting their extra costs, and he was heartily supported by Captains White of Carn Brea, Teague of Tincroft, Hambly of Agar and Bishop of Wheal Grenville.

Dolcoath's old man engine was increasingly regarded as a lethal and obsolescent contraption. Installed back in 1854 and capable of carrying 108 men on a twenty minute journey almost to the bottom of the mine, it had once nearly killed Captain Josiah himself. Holmans had repaired the main beam which broke in 1893 and shortly before being stopped in October 1897, the man engine exacted a final toll; one miner was killed in the morning and another seriously injured during the afternoon. Henceforth men would ride in man cages at Harriet shaft where a new steel headgear and a Holman air compressor had been erected.

Dolcoath's familiar Cornish headgear also vanished and by the spring of 1896 a new steel

One of the many steam winders built by Holmans for a variety of customers in the years before 1914, and which were exported to mines as far away as Mexico and India.

Dolcoath, 'Queen of the Cornish Mines' was always a good customer for Holmans who were in the later days also very large shareholders. Here miners stand beside the Harriet air compressor house while behind them, smoke streams from the stack of the new and much bigger compressor and prominent are the tall steel colliery headframes erected by Holmans during the modernisation of the mine in 1897.

colliery-type headgear towered above New Sump Shaft. Built by Holmans to the designs of Charles Morgans of Cardiff Mining consultants T. W. Morgans who were now consulting engineers at Dolcoath, it was erected in less than a month. They scrapped the old Cornish beam whim that hoisted from New Sump Shaft and replaced it with a small Welsh colliery winder made redundant by the closure of Botallack. After inspection by R. Arthur Thomas, it had been bought from the Holman cousins and brought to Dolcoath behind a traction engine.

Another new steel headgear was erected on Old Sump Shaft while there were more developments over on Straypark, where Holman contract sinkers were putting down the shaft and driving levels despite very hard ground. The Holmans also refitted the ancient Straypark 64 inch pumping engine which, having been re-bored once by Harveys, was now re-bored again and fitted with new gear and boilers.

Perhaps unnerved by this great wave of modernisation Michael Williams, famed for his remarks that he failed to see *'What dividends had to do with profits'*, finally resigned as chairman of Dolcoath after forty years. Frank Harvey, chairman of Harvey's of Hayle, was elected in his place and the vacant seat was filled by James Miners Holman who joined his brother on the board.

The new William's Shaft, was beset by problems from the outset as the weather remained bad for months. Doubts increased that the shaft was far too big, especially when the sinkers struck granite that was either very hard or badly faulted and struggled to cut the shallow adit to help drain the sump. Work was suspended for some time and when it resumed it was obvious that a replacement was needed for the small sinking winder supplied by John Wild & Sons of Oldham in 1895. The old style Cornish beam whim, such as Holmans had erected at East Pool in 1887, would have been enormous and cumbersome, especially as any headgear and machinery would be crowded together on the steep side of Carn Entral.

There was the additional problem of keeping the vast length of wire rope coiled centrally on the winding drum while hoisting from such a depth but a 'daring and original' solution was offered by Charles Morgans, of the same company that worked on the modernisation of Dolcoath. The engine and drum were mounted on a girder bed which itself rode on 16 paired bogie wheels travelling on steel rails, set at 90 degrees to the shaft. The whole 120 tons moved 16 feet laterally for every 1000 feet of wire rope, which always remained coiled centrally over the drum.

Holmans undertook the work, including the 60 foot lattice steel head gear and by February 1900

Williams Shaft on the steep side of Carn Entral was an attempt to rationalise hoisting and hauling in Dolcoath by installing a new winder and a remarkable steel lattice headgear, built by Holmans to the designs of Welsh consulting engineers. Work began in 1895 and would continue for another ten years, and though the equipment was regarded as a technological wonder, the shaft was an expensive failure, and was soon described by the 'Mining Journal' as a 'White Elephant'.

Hoisting from William's shaft was done by a remarkable traversing winding engine, which to keep the 3,000 feet of wire rope always pulling centrally, the whole 120 tons of steel and cast iron, moved from side to side on railway wheels. After twenty years of work the engine was left derelict in the imposing granite house until broken up for scrap in 1938.

With their reliance upon foreign business Holmans had a long tradition of attending exhibitions throughout the world and won two gold medals at the Paris Exposition in 1900. Among the rock drills and mining equipment was (at far right) a working steam model of the famous traversing winding engine they installed at Williams Shaft Dolcoath but this splendid item vanished after the closure of the Holman Museum in 1980.

the sinking crews were ready to begin. However, although the engine *'was being erected and the pit head gear ought to be very soon'* James Holman admitted they were late as strikes up country had delayed material for the foundry. Captain Josiah Thomas was absent, this being the first Dolcoath meeting he had missed in thirty five years, but he wrote to recommend that they have a new air compressor capable of driving 20 drills. This was more than he required but guaranteed the power needed to develop the mine westwards towards Straypark.

By August 1901 the new winder had been installed and tested and the wire ropes were being wound onto the drums and, according to Frank Harvey the chairman, in *'two or three days the contractors would be at work in the shaft sinking rapidly'*. A one sixth scale model of the winder had been made by Holmans for their stand at the Paris Exposition in September 1900. There they won two gold medals for their display of rock drills which were already in use on the South African gold mines. Also on their imposing stand was a 'Duplex' pump, a portable headgear used widely in Australia and West Africa and a patent filter able to supply water for drinking or a boiler. George Batten, the Dolcoath director who visited the exposition, noticed that the model *'caused great interest and curiosity amongst people who included many high officials and who expressed a wish to see it at Dolcoath when it was in full work'*. An extra visitor to the Exposition was seven year old Arthur Trevena Holman, always known in later life as 'Mr Treeve', who travelled across under the care of Mr Smith, the celebrated manager of Holmans' London office at East Acton.

William's Shaft never really fulfilled expectations and when temporarily suspended again through a shortage of funds in 1905, was even then being referred to as an *'expensive white elephant'* by the 'Mining Journal'. R. Arthur Thomas was always reticent about developments at the shaft and an indecisive discussion over the pumping, this led J.H. Collins to claim that questioning him had as much effect as *'a corn plaster on a graven image'*. When sinking was resumed Dolcoath, much to Holman's chagrin, hired Piggott's, the Welsh pit sinkers who used the German 'Flottman' drills which Holmans had regularly beaten in contests in South Africa. The shaft finally bottomed out at 300 feet in May 1910 at a cost of £90,362, which included the remarkable winder.

The race for modernisation brought Holmans further customers when the run of old mines along the Great Lode, between Troon and Carnkie, amalgamated as the Basset Mines in January 1896. They were commanded by Major Frank Oats of St. Just who, like R. Arthur Thomas of Dolcoath, had been converted to mechanised mining by his experience in South Africa. He needed a new winder to hoist from Marriot's Shaft, where it would work alongside an enormous compound engine which, he hoped, would cope with the ocean of water that daily accumulated in the workings. This compound engine was designed by Henry Davey, an engineer of Cornish descent, who was working for Hathorn & Davey's 'Sun' foundry in Leeds at the time. Nicholas Trestrail, the Cornish consulting engineer, issued tenders for a winder to hoist double skips raising 1000 tons a day from a shaft that might reach 5000 feet. Holmans beat off fierce competition and, for £3,600, produced a horizontal compound winder which *'incorporated all the modern appliances for speed power and efficiency'*. It had cylinders of 23 ins and 38 ins, a stroke of 5ft 6in and was equipped with fast-acting 'Corliss' valves, the winder also had massive conical winding drums, themselves an innovation in Cornwall. Holmans also erected the massive steel headgear, which cost three times as much as the old Cornish type headgear that was already fast disappearing.

James Miners Holman proudly informed the 'Mining World' that he was *'making the biggest compound winding engine that has ever been put up in the county'* when they interviewed him at Holman's new London office where A. H. Smith, formerly estimator at Camborne, was the representative. Since they had spoken to him, the works had doubled in size to cope with orders for rock drills and mining machinery. The boiler works had been expanded and the moulding shop extended. He had also taken over the old foundry near the railway station and was converting it into an apprentice training school where, under the instruction of skilled men, the lads would be taught to make small engines and light work before graduating to the main works.

The new winding system at Basset was not infallible, as on one Christmas Eve everybody *'was rushing to leave work early and the driver steamed the engine a little too far. The cage with two full wagons went up the headgear and broke off at the chains...'*. The cage dropped back down the shaft, travelling so fast that no one saw it, and was eventually found 260 fathoms below, having sliced through eight feet of timber, crushed into the slump where it stayed until sinking was resumed years later.

Holmans made a similar smaller hoist for the restarted Gooninis Mine near St. Agnes but the next real masterpiece came after 'Major Frank' returned with another order. As well as having considerable interests in the Basset Mines, he was also one of the largest shareholders at Levant. At the turn of the century this mine was still notorious for its obdurate, often eccentric management and obsolescent equipment. He had campaigned to modernise the mine and a big coupled air winch was installed on the 260 to hoist from the deepening levels. The old Harvey compressor hidden in a shed behind the engine house was inadequate and in June 1899 Captain White insisted that they *'must have a new compressor if they were to open up the mine'*, while the miners *'believed they would be able to do one third more work if they had air at higher pressure'*.

The Holmans were already assembling a massive cross compound stage compressor for Dolcoath. It had Meyer valve gear and an 18 ton flywheel , the *'largest ever made in the moulding shop'*. This would enable R.Arthur Thomas to centralise the air supply, which relied upon five compressors scattered between Wheal Harriet and Valley shaft. It would also save the mine 100 tons of coal a month. Without much prompting from the Holman cousins at St. Just, the Levant committee went to Holmans, who were determined that the new compressor would be the *'best piece of machinery that had ever been turned out of their works'*. It was double the size of that supplied to

Carn Brea and the Hyderabad Mines only a few years before and, unlike the new one for Dolcoath, was driven by a triple expansion jet condensing steam engine equipped with Meyer steam expansion gear. The tandem air cylinders could draught over 3000 cubic feet of *'Free air'* per minute and supply through the receiver 20 rock drills at 80 PSI. The compressor was over 60 feet long and 16 feet wide, with steam being supplied by two Lancashire Boilers.

While the foundry *put their best energies* into making the enormous compressor, John found the opportunity to begin his palatial new villa at Camborne Veor, which lay midway between No.3 works and his brother's house at *'Tregenna'* in Pendarves Road. He was already a widely respected businessman and J.P. and soon brother James was also sworn in as a J.P. at Bodmin. By June, James was travelling across Canada and the U.S.A. to seek business in the mining fields of British Columbia, accompanied by Capt. William Bennetts of the Roskear Fuse Works.

All work ceased on 26 October 1901 when Captain Josiah Thomas was buried in Centenary Chapel *'from whose pulpit of which his voice was so often heard'*. Ten thousand people lined the streets as his coffin was carried from the mine, borne by the six captains at Dolcoath. The cortege was led by Frank Harvey, the chairman, Gilbert Pearce and James Miners Holman. They were followed by the clerks and time keepers and Thomas Morgan of the Welsh engineering company, then 800 tin miners, marching silently and respectfully. It was an extraordinary event, never accorded to any other man in Cornwall, and marked the passing of the last great figure from Cornwall's golden era of hard rock mining.

The christening ceremony for the new Levant compressor, which took place on 22 December 1901, was reminiscent of those once reserved for the starting of some big Cornish pumping engine. To escape a typical wet and stormy day on the Pendeen cliffs, everybody crowded into the magnificent house where they were shown over the compressor by John and James Holman, Nicholas Trestrail and Mr Plummer, Holmans Chief designer. Major White, the doyen of Levant, gallantly offered the honour of starting her up to Major Frank Oats and the compressor *'went off as smoothly as a clock and was the subject of general admiration and satisfaction'*. Toasts were drunk in the special punch brewed by Major White, who proposed *'Success to the Compressor'*. Frank Oats was slightly overwhelmed by its sheer size and power, which was far more than was required at present and it was now up to the Levant agents to ensure they used its power to develop the mine.

The magnificent ruin of compressor house though attacked by 'Stone robbers' over the decades still stands as tribute to the Holmans of Camborne.

John Holman claimed the compressor was faultless in every way, despite intense inspection by a bevy of engineers inside and out. James Holman was rather more lyrical, commenting *'a good compressor was like a good picture it needed a good frame and they had every reason to be pleased at the manner which the Levant company provided the frame'*. He referred to the magnificent compressor house with its tiled floor and 100 foot ornate chimney with its gothic concrete cupola. It comprised 2000 tons of masonry which had cost a pound a ton, enraging many shareholders who resented this expensive *'elaborativeness'*. Indeed, when Nicholas Trestrail submitted his bill for erecting the compressor, the Levant committee reduced it by £17 and dismissed him.

George Plummer, Holmans chief designer who had worked with Nicholas Trestrail, considered the compressor superior to any he had seen in Germany or America and he had worked *'with some of the best engines in the country'*. With proper care and maintenance she would still be at work in twenty years, without fear of ending on the scrap heap. A new feature was noticed by Capt. Willams, home from South Africa. On each side of the bed were cast the words *'Manufactured by Holman Brothers of Camborne'*. The day ended with a response by Mr Holman Jnr. which brought cheers, most certainly Treve Holman, who over thirty years later would be instrumental in saving the small steam winder at Levant's for posterity. Sadly, George Eustice, the consultant engineer, had died on 3 December 1901, only a few weeks before the ceremony.

The Holman boys were always proud of their roots in the Industrial Revolution and just a week after the Levant ceremony, John led the parade of traction engines, miners and engineers in celebration of the centenary of Richard Trevithick's road locomotive going up Camborne Hill on Christmas Eve 1801. He and J.J. Berringer, the chairman of Camborne School of Mines where he was vice governor, spent months organising the parade. It began, on an appropriately wet and rough afternoon, from the presumed site of Tyack's Smithy in Tehidy Road and ended in the main square, opposite the ornate fountain which John Snr had erected in 1889. Amongst the scores of marchers was none other than James McCulloch, still the engineering nomad and about to quit Tuckingmill foundry where he had been developing the 'Little Hercules' Rock Drill for several years.

The Holman boys now employed over a 100 men and were making 1000 rock drills per year besides general mining equipment. Their contract rock drillers were kept busy, though occasionally this caused trouble in mines where they were also shareholders. An irate shareholder at East Pool, faced by heavy losses, asked why they had to

The air compressor built for Levant Mine was a masterpiece of Holman engineering but its sheer cost and that of large and ornate house on Pendeen cliffs was regarded as far too extravagant by the shareholders. The mine never developed sufficiently to take full advantage of the magnificent compressor, which was scrapped around 1920 and replaced by one driven by electric motors.

No.3 Rock Drill works was built on the site of the old Jenkin's foundry, and remained the hub of rock drill production and development for almost fifty years. The handsome brick and granite facade still stands beside the railway station at Camborne but the huge letters have long since vanished.

employ Holmans when they could buy their own machines. John Holman brusquely told him that *'..as long as his firm were makers of rock drills, they would be contractors... We have been asked to contract in South African mines, again and again.... Whether you contract again in East Pool is immaterial to us, because we would rather sell you the machines than contract'.*

As mining agents, Holmans still recruited men for foreign mining fields. *'Wanted. A good rock drill man for six months. Knowledge of Spanish and Holman Drills essential'* was a typical advert. Edward Rowe who went to Margrahamore in Ireland to install *'a Holman steam drill'* was asked to stay as Captain and received a presentation on leaving. Holmans own mineral dressing plant and pneumatic stamps established a world wide reputation hence, *'Wanted for Bolivia. First Class Tin Dresser. Apply with references to Holman Bros. Camborne'.*

Business was so brisk that new machine tools were regularly added, as in December 1903 when Thomas Ward of Sheffield sold off the remaining machinery at Harvey's foundry. Holmans bought a variety of centre lathes including, for £200, a big hexagon turret lathe by Alfred Herbert of Coventry. An 8 ton ladle for the foundry cost £15 and a wrought iron jib crane slightly more, with a steam hammer being procured for £92 *'prompt cash'*. A punching and angle cutting machine cost them £40 and an air receiver just £18.

The closure of Harveys Foundry had benefited Holmans, who employed many of the redundant young apprentices and skilled men. William Rodda came to Cornwall from Cheshire in 1890 and moved to Camborne three years later. After a spell at 'Climax' he joined Holmans in 1897, becoming one of the original team who set up the new No.3 Rock drill works. Joseph Tromans began his career as a chain maker at Cradley Heath. When the Harvey Foundry declined he brought his family to Camborne in 1884, at the invitation of James Miners Holman, providing he could have a house. He spent the next thirty years in the smiths shop while his son Thomas, aged fifteen, who had worked alongside him at Harveys, spent the next sixty years as faggoter, smith and tool sharpener. The Tromans family produced many good musicians including Thomas, who was a founder of the famous Holman

Male Voice Choir. Thomas's son Percy would eventually become manager of the No.1 Works.

There were still orders for big compressors and another one was being made for Carn Brea and Tincroft when a young apprentice pattern maker joined the company on 30 April 1904, the *'patterns were being made and some of the castings were well advanced. There were no draughtsmen in my early days. The compressor was marked out in pencil on a big whitened board which was practically the length of the pattern shop. Then later, drawings were made from the finished parts. The compressor was too big for us to assemble at the works. When Mr Plummer joined, the old system got a shaking. He introduced the idea of preparing drawings BEFORE the manufacture of engines and so on. Before then, the practice had been the other way round. Plummer came to the works in a silk hat. Never missed.'* In December 1906 East Pool contracted with Holmans for a new compressor to be delivered in twelve months but *'owing to the expeditious way the company always carries out its contracts, the compressor has not only been delivered and placed in position (June 3rd 1907) but is practically ready to start work'.*

No big 'Cornish' pumping engines had been built since the closure of Harvey of Hayle but Holman Brothers had the distinction of making the very last of them. In January 1903, the Dorothea Slate Quarry in North Wales decided to install a large pumping engine to cope with a serious inrush of water. Nicholas Trestrail was asked to inspect two old 'Seventies' lying in Cornwall but neither was suitable. Accordingly he was asked to design a new 'Sixty Eight' capable of working 18 inch pumpwork. Holmans tender for £1,925 was accepted while the Redruth Foundry were contracted to cast the heavy pitwork.

The machine shop at No.3 Rock Drill Works at the turn of the century crowded with lathes, mills and drills, a scene that would not drastically change, apart from belt drives being replaced by electric motors, until the advent of computerised technology.

A Holman drifter, mounted on a tripod, which had been loaned to their St.Just cousins, at work on the foreshore under Newlyn Quarry in May 1904

Nicholas Trestrail's *'Plan of Pitwork'* was received at Dorothea on 25 April 1904 and the *'Big Shaft'* was prepared to receive the new engine. The 82 tons of pitwork, apart from two long lengths of rising main and a windbore sent on by rail, was shipped onboard the Bideford Ketch *'Iron King'* which sailed from Hayle on 3 September 1904, arriving at Canarvon five days later. The 'Bob' was despatched on a G.W.R. flat car from the yard of No.1.on 14 October 1914. Six days later the quarry manager noted that the *'Big Beam of the new engine arrived at Nantille Station from Messrs Holman Bros. of Camborne Cornwall, through Mr Trestrail. Weight 22 tons 12 cwt. A traction engine belonging to Mr Robert Roberts of Abergele arrived to haul the heavy parts to the quarry.'*

During the following week the rest of the engine arrived from Camborne which was duly noted.

October 21st	*Unloading Big beam at station'*
October 25th	*Cylinder bottom, weighing 5 tons 11 cwts. Cylinder Cover weighing 3 tons 10 cwts and Piston and Rings weighing 2 tons 198 cwt 3 qurs, were hauled from station to quarry.*
Oct 26th	*Big beam was hauled to Quarry.*
Oct 28th	*Cylinder arrived at station weighing 16 tons 17 cwts 1 qur.*
Oct 29th	*Hauling cylinder to the quarry.*

Holman Bros. made very few Cornish pumping engines including the handsome 68 inch for the Dorothea Slate quarry Engine in North Wales, which was erected in April 1906. and is seen here pausing during the dinner hour in August 1951, not long before she finally ceased work,

Evidently the rough weather considerably delayed operations and not until 4 April 1905 was it recorded that *'Thos. Rowe arrived from Cornwall to superintend the erection of the engine'*. Next day, having been joined by his son Percy, they began *'Rising the Bed plate of Big beam to the top of the front wall'*. On the 17th they were engaged *'Lifting Big Beam to its place'*; ten days later were busy *'lifting and fixing the cylinder'* and on 15 June 1905 *'Thos Rowe and his son left for home after finish erecting the engine'*.

There was another long delay but on 5 Feb 1905 *'George Perry "Pitman"* arrived at the quarry from Cornwall to superintend the fixing of pumps'. Manoeuvring and adjusting the heavy cast iron work in the cramped shaft was a laborious task, though Perry used a capstan engine from a Victorian battleship lately scrapped by Thos Ward of Sheffield. On 8 May 1906 Thomas Rowe was back *'from Cornwall to start the engine'*. and four days later the *'new engine moved for the first time, in order to take away some props that were holding the rising main'*. On 14th May the *'new engine and pumps starting to work for the first time'* and Nicholas Trestrail soon arrived to check the work. Adjustments were needed but on the 19th *'Thomas Rowe left for Cornwall and W. H. Curnow arrived in order to learn our men how to work the new engine'*. In a month he and George Perry left for Cornwall and the 'New engine began to pump on 19th July 1906'. and would stay in service until replaced by electric pumps fifty years later.

Next year Holmans were asked to build another large Cornish pumping engine, an 'Eighty', again designed by Nicholas Trestrail. This was for the re-working of South Phoenix mine near Liskeard. The bob was fabricated from rolled steel plates by Holmans but the enormous cylinder was sub-contracted to Worsley Meines Foundry of Wigan.

Holmans were still called upon to repair or refurbish some of the few Cornish engines left at work around Camborne. they supplied a new bottom for the cylinder of the 80 inch pumping engine on Lyle's Shaft at the Basset Mines, after the main rod broke and the bob came 'in doors'. One notable job came after the old Harvey 'Bob' of Goold's 'Eighty' at Wheal Grenville, suddenly broke in half at the gudgeons late on a September night in 1906. Six tons of cast iron crashed down on the steps where the engineman and his mate had been sitting just a few minutes before, but was stopped from falling into the shaft by the pumping rod. Immediately there were rumours that the engine was wrecked and the mine flooding but on arrival, the correspondent of the 'Mining Journal' was confronted by Capt. Negus climbing out of the big cylinder and accepted his offer to inspect the damage, which was not that devastating.

Marshall's engine kept the water down while Capt. Negus summoned Holmans engineers, who only a month before had been underground to repair a cracked balance bob in the same shaft. The new bob for the 'Eighty' was 38 tons to the old one's 23 and as a precaution horns were cast on the underside of both ends to anchor steel bridles which would brace a kingpost should the same accident happen again. So urgent was the work that instead of allowing the mass of iron to cool for two or three days the foundrymen made thick gloves from Hessian bags to enable them to free the bob from the casting mould.

The bob was raised by a *'willing gang of Grenville miners'* who worked day and night under Capt. Negus, and were rewarded for their efforts by Peter Watson, the chairman. On 7 Nov 1906 the directors, who found nobody to blame for the accident, heard that *'the new bob which has been cast with greater weight and improvements made thereto - by Holman Brothers Ltd. - has been*

The new bob for Grenville Mine hangs from chains under the overhead crane in the casting shop ready to be despatched in September 1906. Bigger and heavier than the one which had suddenly broke, the bob was hauled to the mine by wagon and winched up onto the 'Bob' Wall' of Goold's engine house by the Grenville miners.

placed in position. The engine was set to work on Saturday last, the 3rd instn. and has continued to work smoothly and satisfactorily during the last week.'

The Grenville bob was a remarkable success for Holmans who already had a new winder in their shops for South Crofty, at that time the newest and ultimately the last of all the Cornish tin mines. A big Cornish pumping engine had been set up in 1903 on the new Robinsons shaft, sunk like Williams at Dolcoath to avoid a maze of old workings and crooked shafts. By 1906 Crofty was controlled by Cornish Consolidated Mines, a speculative and labyrinthine conglomerate of companies relying upon a high tin price mainly to rework long closed tin mines. Surprisingly, South Crofty had defected to 'Climax' after buying 'Little Vixens' and the big 'Imperials', beginning a tradition that would last fifty years. The mine came to Holmans for a new 400 HP steam winder, a 22 inch twin cylinder direct acting horizontal, with double beat drop valves and a 4 ft stroke, driving one fast drum which was permanently keyed to shafting and a second drum that could be clutched in or out. The winder was steamed by two Lancashire boilers and well equipped with a Greens 'Economiser', two Thompson Feed pumps and a Wheeler condenser. During the spring of 1907 foundations for the engine were laid, being *'concrete throughout and not a single one of those granite blocks which formerly gave the old 'loadings' the jumps'. The engineman recorded, 'Started with single cage fixed drum ...8th April 1907'*. By July, the winder was ready to hoist double decker cages on $1\frac{1}{8}$ steel wire at 1000 feet a minute via a new and massive timber headgear mounted on concrete piers. Crofty had also ignored Holmans and erected a big 'Reidler' air compressor together with 2 steel Lancashire boilers, air receiver, cooling tower and reservoir and a 100 steel chimney. Robinson's winder as it quickly became known, would, with various modifications, work uninterrupted for the next fifty years.

In January 1908 Holmans opened their new showroom in Wesley St which attracted a great deal of attention, especially the photograph of *'three huge elephants in the track of a boiler.... two apparently pushing it. The steep mountainside is admirably depicted while on the other side a band of swarthy Orientals are seeing 'Fair Play'*. There were also desplays of drills and another large

Built by Holmans to the order of Captain Josiah Paul of South Crofty Mine, this powerful steam winder, saw sixty years of almost unbroken service, hoisting men, material and rock from Robinson's Shaft. For forty years the engineman was Charlie Buzza, who is seen at the controls shortly before the engine ceased work in May 1967.

photograph showing Coolies hauling a boiler with a Cornishman supervising the operation.

Holmans also had an excellent display at that summer's exhibition at Olympia and brought it all home for the Polytechnic Exhibition held in Camborne Market House during the first week of September. The continuing success of Holman Brothers was sadly interrupted by the death of John Henry Holman at the early age of fifty five at 'Tregenna' on 4 November 1908.

A Boiler being hauled towards a Compressor plant in the early 1900's supplied by Holman Brothers to an Indian Railway Company.

South African miners including many Cornishmen, pose with their Holman rock drills after creating a world record by sinking the main shaft at Kleinfontein Deep Gold Mine, 131 feet during January 1907.

Chapter Four

The Gold Reefs

'I have great pleasure in testifying that during the month of January 1907, at the Kleinfontein Deep Ltd... 131 feet were sunk in 13 drilling rounds..

This I believe constitutes a world record and was performed with your 3 1/4" 'Holman Drills'. This record should establish an undoubted efficiency which you claim for your drills

Benoni Transval.

If the discovery at a Boer farmstead in 1887 had been tin or copper, history might have been different but the strike was gold; the largest deposit in the world and concentrated along a range of low scrubby hills, the 'Ridge of White Water', the Witwatersrand. Henceforth, gold mining and South Africa were indivisible and this was to shape the lives of generations of Cornish miners and engineers.

Imposing granite villas around Camborne and Redruth still echo the days of '*South Africa the Golden*', with names like 'Crown Reef', 'Ferreira Deep' and 'Randfontein' still discernable on marble plaques or faded glass fan lights. After the great tin slump of 1895 the Witwatersrand became the eldorado for every Cornish miner tired of long shifts and poor pay. Baggage and trunks bearing the labels 'Capetown' and 'Johannesburg ' became familiar sights on railway platforms from Penzance to Liskeard, while there was the Friday night ritual of seeing off husbands, fathers and brothers who crowded into carriages whose windows bore the sticker

'Southampton'. 'Union Castle' became to the Witwatersrand what Cunard was to Michigan and 'P & O' was to Kalgoorlie.

Diamonds at Kimberly and gold on the Witwatersrand drew thousands of Cornishmen into South Africa, miners, engineers, artisans and small tradesmen. There was big money to be made; the prudent or the lucky came home and bought themselves a coal yard, grocery store or public house. More transitory and flamboyant was the spectacle on Saturday nights when the '*Africa men*', resplendent in digger hats and gold watch chains, pushed their way through the doors of 'Tabb's Hotel' in Redruth or the 'Commercial' at Camborne, often ending the night sprawled in the gutter or being kicked off the last tramcars.

The Cornish survived all the political upheavals. Cecil Rhodes might have smuggled 200 rifles and a million rounds of ammunition in oil drums to the discontented 'Ouitlanders' in Johannesburg but the Cornish had come to dig gold, not join a revolution against their Boer landlords. They decamped in railway cars carrying the derisive slogans '*For Cornish and kaffirs only*' but many did serve in the Matabele Wars or later when the Boer war itself broke out, though scores came home where Cornish mining had revived, aided by the introduction of electricity.

When the war ended in 1903 the country was in a desperate state, especially after three years of highly effective guerrilla war which had done somewhat less damage than the heavy-handed counter-measures of the British military. The massive reconstruction of the country relied upon the wealth of the Witwatersrand but the mines were in a parlous state when the Boer field armies quit the Rand in the spring of 1900. Only Geldenhuis, which was owned by a neutral French company, had stayed at work and when the British army was advancing, '*Oom Paul*' - Paul Kruger, the Boer president - had threatened to blow up every mine on the Rand, an Armageddon more akin to the Old Testament

The first Holman workshop at Denver Johannesburg around 1914 with a white engineer posing with his assistants including 'John Chinaman' one of the 50,000 Chinese labourers who were shipped to South Africa as temporary solution to the shortage of labour after the Boer War.

A scene familiar to generations of Cornish miners, a Holman drill mounted on a 'Bar and Arm', manned by two machine boys, at work in a gold stope in the 1930's

than the practical application of dynamite to 43 separate mines.

Yet the goldmines were recognised as the salvation of South Africa but they had to be not only refurbished but developed at a pace never before considered. The answer, like that in Cornwall thirty years before, was mechanisation, haulage, winding, stamping and especially machine drilling. The Rand became a Mecca for American, German and English engineering companies, all eager to cater for a market where they stood to make millions. The Holmans themselves were ready for such a boom, especially as the Cornishmen on the Rand were certainly going to make sure the new machines came from home, though their own tin mines were dwarfed by those on the Rand. By 1909 there were 2,389 rock drills boring the gold reefs while 2,000,000 tons of rock were being hoisted to surface. Small wonder that John Holman had hoped one day that they would be '*able to exploit Dolcoath on the lines obtained in South Africa*', though the deepest gold shaft, the Catlin at Jumpers GM., was already 1,000 feet deeper than Williams Shaft.

He had visited the Rand in 1904 accompanied by his wife and two Holmans men, Frank Luke and WJ Trythall, who were to open a stores and workshop in Johannesburg. Soon to follow was young Arthur Reynolds who was from an old St Agnes mining family and the son of the manager of Charlestown Foundry. Tired of a '*sedentary*' clerk's job in No. 3, he chose to try his fortune on the Rand. So successful was he that twenty years later he returned to establish a thriving coal business, supplied by his own steam colliers sailing from Portreath. His young cousin John Reynolds, spent some time at No. 3 before going over to work under Mr Miller at No. 1 until, in 1911, he was transferred to the short lived New York office.

Among Holmans agents were Howard Farrar & Co and the ebullient William Hosken of Hayle or ''B'Losken" to his fellow Cornishmen. He was a pioneer 'Uitlander' who had sat on the 'Reform

Breaking records was a regular event as rock drill companies strove to capture the market on the Witwatersrand, and a typical sinking crew pose with their Holman drills, after putting down the No.1. incline at Brakpan Goldmine during June 1908.

Committee' during the Jamieson Raid back in 1895. He always preferred the turbulent 'politiking' of the Rand to mere storekeeping and a legacy of this was the bundle of dynamite found buried under the porch of his home '*Trelawney*' in Jeppe's town.

James Holman's trip to the Rand was very successful and by early 1905 '*the most satisfactory sounds in the evenings are those of the hammers of Messrs. Holman Bros. No. 3 factory where they are working overtime on a good order from South Africa.*' The 'African World' also carried a long article on the big air compressor at Dolcoath, which appears to be a vigorous reply to the publicity campaign waged by 'Climax' whose adverts easily outshone those of Holmans in the 'Cornish Post ' or 'Mining Journal'.

Yet Climax and all the other makers of mining machinery faced enormous technological challenges out on the Witwatersrand. The goldmines demanded speed and mechanisation and there was no place for the old traditions which encumbered the Cornish mines, though both the Cornish miners and engineers once in South Africa never hesitated to embrace all the new mining methods.

There was a price tag attached to this amazing technological development and that was 'Phthisis', the destruction of a miner's lungs by the dust of the gold stope, hard silicate dust so fine that it could seize the bearings of a theodolite. Drilling, blasting and shovelling was all done 'dry' amidst clouds of dust. The result was catastrophic, especially among the Cornish miners. At one time so many were being buried daily in Bramnfontein Cemetery that they were likened to the Japanese troops, renowned for their suicidal '*Banzai*' charges at the storming of Port Arthur. Soon there was '*scarcely a village in the Duchy which has not seen a victim of this disease*'. Both Holman and 'Climax' produced patent dust allaying water sprays but the Cornish miners were notoriously indifferent. It was to take decades before regulation and development

An engineer stands at the controls of a big Holman diagonal air winch in a level underground in Van Ryn Deep around 1908.

of the rock drill were to reduce the dreadful toll of phthisis.

The great quest was for a small machine to open up the narrow gold stopes as opposed to the enormous reciprocating drifters which, even after twenty years of development, remained great consumers of air, time and manpower. There now ensued almost a repeat of the frantic rivalry between rock drill companies, which had happened in Cornwall 25 years before during the early days of boring machines. To bring order into the chaos of competition, various trials were arranged. The 'South African Mining Journal' sponsored a contest in the winter of 1907 but in a startling result the 'Gordan' drill, made by Ingersoll Sergeant, beat all comers though the American machine did not fulfil expectations in practical use underground.

The South African Chamber of Mines joined the fray when in February 1908 they offered a prize of £2,500 for the best drill that was sufficiently light and small to work the narrow gold stopes. This was doubled by the Transvaal Govt. and a formal competition was organised under strict rules whereby all drills would undergo surface trials at the Transvaal University and then complete 300 shifts, 43 each in a working gold stope. Once the footage and individual costings were established, it was believed that all but the best machine would be eliminated.

Even as the competition was being organised, Holmans claimed another record when their 3 1/4 drills drove a level 226 feet in Cinderella Deep during March 1908. This was quickly followed by another at Brakpan Mine when their big No.1 Incline shaft was sunk 223 feet by Holman drills during June 1908. Such pounding inevitably took its toll of any rock drill, despite the maker's claims. One Randite considered the old Holman tappet machine one '*of the worst he had ever used, especially its patent tapered chuck'*. Unless lined with an old tin can it usually jammed solid at the end of a shift and the only way to free the drill steel was to '*hold the chuck over a fire of old*

3,000 feet under the Witwatersrand at the bottom of Van Ryn Deep, two miners, their 'Baas Boy' and 'Machine Boy' stop for a break alongside a Holman drifter in 1908. Despite the heat and dust, pipes are being happily puffed while the 'Boys' work without the benefit of boots.

candle ends and dynamite boxes;' In desperation one shift boss used a shaving of dynamite to blow the drill steel out of the chuck.

The great 'Stope Drill Contest' began in May 1909 with an added bonus of substantial prizes for the actual miners manning the first, second and third machines. The trials, at Transvaal University and underground in Feirrera Deep, eliminated nine of the nineteen competitors but low air pressure, the curse of the Rand mines, meant the 300 shifts were reduced to 217 and the competition was extended by a further six months. The struggle waged back and forth in the gold stopes of Crown Deep, Village Deep and Robinson Deep, with the laurels for the best machine being reluctantly relinquished each time some other machine bored deeper and faster.

The marathon competition was keenly followed back in Cornwall, though the partisans of both 'Climax' and Holmans had to share the 'Cornish Pavillion' at the 'Imperial Exhibition' held at White City during the summer of 1909. This was a glittering showcase for Cornish industry with the Prince of Wales as patron and well supported by the mining gentry and mineral landlords. All the big firms displayed their products. Holman showed a variety of their drills, air cushion stamps and the popular stretcher bar hoists, which were being used in 100 mines in Africa and Australia, 'Climax' had their 'Imperial' Rock drill and Tuckingmill Foundry, the 'Little Hercules'. National Explosives and Bickford Smith mounted large displays while every working Cornish mine sent minerals and ores. R. Arthur Thomas eclipsed them all with a model of Carn Brea Monument cast in solid gold to represent the total value of tin and copper raised during the long career of Dolcoath Mine. Flanking this amazing work of art was a big ebonised case full of Dolcoath minerals and a large pile of ingots of Cornish tin from the Williams Harvey smelter. Sadly the monument has not survived for posterity and neither did the beautiful bowl made by the Newlyn Art Classes from silver raised from the Perran Mine during 1908. James Miners Holman who been travelling with his wife in Egypt for the past two months arrived home in time to attend the 'Cornish Day' at White City which, held on the lawn in bright sunshine and hosted by Lord and Lady Falmouth, was a splendidly Cornish occasion.

The 'Great Stope Drill Trial' was finally won by Holmans whose 2 $^{1}/_{8}$, after a rigorous 12 months of testing, drilled 12,779 inches at a cost of barely 10 pence a foot, then half the cost of black labour. The cheque was presented by the Minister of Mines for the Transvaal in September 1910, just after six Holman 3 $^{1}/_{4}$ inch machines excelled their past records by sinking a 20 ft. by 8 ft. incline shaft 279 feet in a month at Van Ryn Deep.

The two competition drills were shipped home and displayed at the Polytechnic Society Exhibition where it was noted that '*the Rand dust is still upon them.*' Holman gained a Diploma of Honour but back on the Rand, Climax soon claimed a record for their 'Imperial' drill for single handed driving a level in New Primrose and this was not the last of the rivalry between the two companies.

The gold mines of the Witwatersrand would remain one of Holmans best customers for decades, although they continued to export mining machinery around the world. In May 1905 their 3 $^{1}/_{2}$ inch drills sank the main shaft of the Murchison Mine in Australia 81 feet in a month through very hard diorite, despite

A Holman air winch working a 'scraper', which scraped broken rock from the stope or levels saving enormous amounts of laborious shovelling and tramming.

stoppages for pumping and timbering. Holman stamps were installed, at a £1000 less than a Californian battery, at the Mountain Queen Mine in Western Australia as part of a massive crushing complex with a 150 ton ore bin, sieve loaders, and line shafting mounted on tall concrete pillars; the whole operation being housed in a huge galvanised shed.

The continuing success and increased expansion of the Camborne business had led the Holman Brothers to convert to a private limited company in 1906, with themselves as sole directors. Unfortunately John, the senior director, was already very seriously ill and in the following year James's son John Leonard Holman, who had just finished his apprenticeship under the redoubtable Nicholas Curry, joined the board. "Mr Leonard" was soon dispatched on a worldwide business trip and in 1910 alone he visited Mexico, the U.S.A. and Canada. However, he was home in September to marry Gladys Fredericka Thomas, daughter of C. Fred Thomas and granddaughter of the great Capt. Josiah Thomas of Dolcoath and whose mother was from the Bartle family of iron founders.

October 1910 saw the closure of the Tuckingmill Foundry, once the lair of James McCulloch, after sixty years. The Holmans do not appear to have attended the three-day auction, though they must have derived a certain satisfaction when his 'Little Hercules' drills were sold off cheaply in batches. Many of the skilled men and apprentices, like those who came from Harvey's, were happily re-employed by Holmans. William Yoe started at the age of thirteen in the moulding shop at Tuckingmill, then spent six years at James Hosking's Foundry which was demolished to make for Holmans new rockdrill works and, after working at Roseworthy Hammer Mills, joined No.3. in 1911. Charles Blewett was originally a Harvey apprentice who graduated to Tuckingmill before joining Holmans No.3. in 1911. After leaving Roskear School, Jack Powning served at Tuckingmill until joining No 3. where his first job was assembling and testing new cradle hammer drills for America, and he would spend the next fifty years with Holmans. Another Tuckingmill

At the suggestion of some expatriate Cornish engineers and mine captains Holmans produced the 'Stretcher Bar Hoist', a small but powerful air hoist that could be mounted on a column like a rock drill. Hundreds like this one seen at work in Dolcoath around 1910, were exported to Australia and South Africa.

apprentice was Charles Trezona Phillips who, once time served, migrated to the U.S.A. There, he spent some years as an improver in a Railway Locomotive shop at Duluth, Minnesota before returning home to join Holmans as a lathe operator and then going over to No. 3.

In 1911 James Holman acquired a more palatial residence, 'Rosewarne House' which was built in 1773 by the Harris family of Camborne. Their eldest son William was a contemporary of Richard Trevithick, whose famous Road Locomotive ran past the gates of 'Rosewarne' on Christmas Eve 1901. Eventually 'Rosewarne' came to an only daughter who, having made an unhappy marriage, settled into an increasingly eccentric old age with her backward son and the estate eventually fell into Chancery. James Holman restored the house to its Georgian elegance and where the grounds faced Tehidy Road, an imposing stone wall soon replaced a crumbling hedge with an impressive new house and iron gates made at No.1.

James Holman's continuing prosperity reflected that of the works which already had a wide reputation of improvement and innovation. Story has it that while homeward bound from South Africa he was joined in the steamer's saloon by some mining engineers and Cornish '*Capns*' returning from Australia. They discussed improvements to machinery and he was asked, '*Why don't you build a hoist light enough to clamp on a simple drill column and powerful enough to hoist 500 to 1000 pound*'. The result was the Holman 'Stretcher Bar Hoist' which weighed just a little more than the 3 1/4 drifter, was driven by either single or double air cylinders and could be erected in very cramped places. The new hoist was soon widely used, especially in Australia.

There were still plenty of orders for big steam winders like that supplied to the Pachuca Mines in Mexico, home of generations of Cornish miners. Captain Josiah Paull of South Crofty, a mere fortnight after ordering two self dumping skips, accepted Holman's tender for a paired 22 inch cylinder steam hoist with a 48 ins stroke, complete with two 8 ft by 3 ft winding drums, drop valve gear, cage indicator and foot operated

The production line of air winches in the No.1 erection shop around 1910

Built in 1906 the impressive granite and gothic Holman head office, was used until the company shifted to 'Rosewarne' House forty years later, and continued to dominate Camborne until demolished to make way for a supermarket in 1990.

A portrait of James Miners Holman commands the Board Room, which is plain and workman like, with solid furniture, though the walls are covered with some excellent paintings and photographs.

brakes. He requested that '*Delivery to be made to New Cook's Shaft and the services of a skilled erector to be provided ... We are prepared to increase the time required for delivery to five months providing you will accept this date under a penalty clause of 1 % per week.*' The new hoist took slightly longer and not until 1 April 1914 could Capt. Paull record that '*the erection of the new winding engine is well in hand and we hope to resume sinking operations by May 1st.*' A week later, the new winder was baling out the shaft with water skips ready for the work.

Holman had also recently supplied East Pool with a new air compressor capable of draughting 1200 C.F.M. and driven by a 215 H.P. Westinghouse electric motor. This was fed by the grid of the Cornish Electric power Co. whose new power station at Hayle had resulted in an '*Electric Boom*' amongst Cornish Industry. By January 1913, Grenville Mine was building the foundations for its own Holman compressor, driven by a 230 HP motor by the Lancaster Dynamo Co. Both compressors were to meet up in their later careers.

Holmans also managed one old time job when the bob of the stamps engine at Wheal Kitty near St. Agnes suddenly broke on Friday 13th. May 1913. A new one was ordered that same evening and left the yard of No.1. works at 11 am just eight days later. At 10.30 am on 25 June the bob was raised into position, which J H Collins, the doyen of Cornish mining, considered '*a fine piece of repairing work, which I think holds the record for work of this class... and a great credit is due to Messers Holman'.*

The company calendar for 1913 celebrated their achievements world wide with the painting '*Evening in a Cornish valley*' by Garstain Cox, Ben Cock's nephew, who at only twenty-one was maturing into a superb artist. He was a rare being, a native Cornish artist, whose roots were in the

'*Black Country*' around Camborne. His father Willam Cox was not only chief draughtsman for Holmans but also an exceptional artist himself, who had many friends among the Newlyn School of painters. Indeed, he named his son after the celebrated painter Norman Garstain. The young Garstain Cox had studied at the Camborne School of Arts and later with John Noble Barber of the St. Ives School. His magnificent Cornish landscapes and seascapes were shown at the Royal Academy and when they were portrayed on the Holman calendars, were pinned on walls by 'Cousin Jacks' in mining camps all over the world.

There was also a visit from Monsieur Kinsman, a French Safety Fuse maker who was somewhat overwhelmed as he found that '*by the means of a splendid array of machine tools, each of which cost some hundreds of pounds.... which enables them to turn out from 80 to 100 complete drills and spare parts per week. Many of their machines are automatic, and men machines work rapidly in ideal conditions as regards light - air and space. A part can be made to a thousandth of an inch. At their No. 1 Foundry I learned that having settled in their new offices they are gradually demolishing all the factory in the square leading west to Centenary Chapel, and that this will be covered with new buildings, all the present yard space being roofed over, so that in making pnuematic stamps, winches, air compressors, and other heavy machinery, the conditions will be as modern and efficient as at their rock drill works*'.

It was a splendid accolade for Holman Bros. Ltd., who never seemed more prosperous or bustling, while the family's ordinary business was supplemented by an extraordinary share portfolio. Besides Malayan tin fields, Brazilian gold mines and Cornish utilities and banks, it also embraced such novelties as the Red Sea Phosphate Co. and the San Paulo Tramway, Light & Power Co. Yet within a year much was to change and a new era was about to begin for the company.

Holmans exported their mining machinery to some of the most remote and inaccessible mining camps in the world, like this tin dressing and crushing plant which has been erected high in the Bolivian Andes, much in the fashion as Trevithick did with Nicholas Holman's boilers a hundred years before.

THE JAMES

PATENT

ORE CONCENTRATING TABLES

CATALOGUES OF "HOLMAN" SPECIALITIES IN ORE CRUSHING AND DRESSING PLANT
WILL BE FORWARDED ON APPLICATION.

MANUFACTURERS & SELLING AGENTS of JAMES PATENT CONCENTRATING TABLES
FOR THE WORLD
EXCLUDING THE UNITED STATES, CANADA & NEW ZEALAND.

Holman Brothers, Ltd.,

Camborne, England.

TELE. & CABLE: AIRDRILL, CAMBORNE.
TELEPHONE NO. 75 AND 76. (2 LINES)

LONDON OFFICE: BROAD STREET HOUSE, E.C., 2.
TELE. & CABLE:—AIRDRILL AVE, LONDON.
TELEPHONE NO. 9270, LONDON WALL.

A heavy Radial drill, set up to drill bolt holes in the mortar box of a stamps, a machine and a method of working that had not radically altered when the author did the same job in 'P.T.' fifty years after this during the 1960's.

'Shell girls' at their lathes in No.3 Rock Drill works during 1918.

Chapter Five

World war one

"The splendid response of the many hundreds of girls who in our rock drill department alone took the place of over two hundred skilled men, was a factor of considerable importance"

' What we did during the Great War'.

The momentous year of 1914 began splendidly for Holman Bros. Ltd with a full order book, especially for the Rand. Other machinery and drills were also due to be shipped out to India, China and Russia. 108 South African mines and 104 Australian mines used air, steam or electric hoists which could be adapted for pumping as well as winding. Holman's new catalogue reflected their energy and adaptability as, following complaints from British Consuls that only the German companies produced publicity in foreign languages, they published another catalogue in Spanish, fully illustrated and on fine art paper. Two '*Holman Scholarships*' worth £100 per year were created for boys attending the Camborne elementary schools, the company providing an ordinary apprentice wage for five years and the fees for attending the Mining school. The company also found the opportunity to exhibit their latest rock drills at the Anglo American Exposition held in London during July 1914, where the model of William Murdoch's tiny steam '*Flyer*' was also exhibited.

Of enormous importance to all the manufacturers of rock drills was that 1914 saw the end of the patent on the American Leyner drill, which had gone a long way towards solving the underground dust problem. George Leyner was a Colorado farm

A rare aerial view of the Cornwall Drop Stamping Co.'s, works or 'Boiler Works as it was always known, lying at the terminus of the Roskear G.W.R. Roskear branch Line, which went through the main works a mile away. Close by the works is a large open shaft belonging to old North Roskear Mine, which according to legend was repository of a wide variety of unwanted articles.

boy turned engineer who, after considerable experimentation, invented the '*water tube*', which would become a universal feature of all rock drills. A small diameter steel tube was designed to pass down through the centre line of all the interior components - like the piston - until it located in a similar hole in the centre of the drill steel itself. Water pumped down the tube turned the dust into a sludge that trickled out of the borehole.

The expansion of No.3 Works saw rock drill production being almost doubled, while down at the Cornwall Boiler Works, a new oil fired furnace capable of bringing a two inch bar to white heat in a few minutes had been installed. There was a battery of big hammers, including a 12 cwt die headed which once tripped '*One, two, three, the result was a flattened pad which would later form part of a rock drill*'. Parted off under the cutting hammer, the steel was de-frazed by a press '*leaving in the tongs a red hot but finished drop forging*'.

John Warren, the manager, was extremely proud of his new machinery which cut working time from hours to minutes and was capable of producing 200 forgings a day, making Boiler Works one of the most modern works outside of the Midlands. He was a stern and exacting engineer who was driven back and forth to work each day in a pony trap by a young lad who would himself join the works. Fifty years later he recalled that a gentleman who wanted a completed boiler delivered to Hayle, on being asked how he wished to pay, opened up an *'old green bag'* full of shining gold sovereigns. Another boiler contract for Hayle provoked the anticipated storm from John Warren when he discovered that the company concerned had shut without cancelling the order.

The next generation of Holman boys, like their fathers before them, had joined the family tradition that extended from boardroom to shop floor. That is with the exception of John's son Jack, a splendid and happy young man who, after leaving Blundell's College at Tiverton, had chosen a military career and gone off to Sandhurst. In September 1913 he was gazetted a Lieutenant in the 4th Royal Irish Dragoon Guards and was posted to Dublin, enjoying the polo playing life of a young officer.

Treve Holman was an energetic and athletic twenty year old who, like many young men with a mechanical bent, was captivated by the new art of flying. Having failed to get airborne because of rough weather at Hendon in 1911, he went aloft with the French aviator Gustave Salmet, who thrilled crowds by flying from the Eastern Green beach at Penzance in May 1914. Circling St. Michael's Mount at 1400 feet was also Treve's way of celebrating that he had just been elected to the Board of Holmans.

Treve Holman eventually managed to go flying at Hendon but was disappointed when the pilot mistook his waving to go higher as a signal to descend. He did fly again during the hot summer days of June 1914 when the young Irish earl Lord Carberry, the '*Flying Earl*', brought his 80 hp. Morane to Sinns Barton Farm near Redruth. Kenneth, Treve and Leonard willingly paid their five guineas for a flight, as did Miss Dorothy, Leonard's sister, but only one gentleman from Penzance was prepared to pay the thirty guineas to loop the loop.

James Miners Holman himself, as chairman of East Pool, was attempting to settle an acrimonious dispute between the committee and the miners over reform of working hours and payment of wages. Holman had known for a long time that such a big and relatively modern mine could not survive under the old 'Cost Book' system and that it would have to be replaced by a limited company. Accordingly he had invited W.C. Moreing of Bewick Moreing, a large mining consultancy, to join the board and help carry through the change over. Their partnership saved East Pool and James Holman's daughter Dorothy actually married Captain Algernon Moreing, who became an M.P. for the Mining Division.

In the spring of 1914 the situation was worsened by the sudden collapse of the over inflated tin market, which sank the ephemeral empire of Cornish Consolidated Tin Mines and almost all of their highly expensive reworking of old Cornish mines. A lot of Holman machinery soon went up for auction, including the big air compressor at Botallack and the 400 hp cross compound winder, built for the 1909 exhibition and installed with 6 head of pneumatic stamps at Great Dowgas Mine. At South Phoenix Mines the 80 inch pumping engine, christened so hopefully by the Prince of Wales, went out of steam for good while, in June 1914, 'Batters' Eighty' ceased work at Great Condurrow. Few realised she would end up as assorted scrap iron in the foundry furnaces at Holmans.

The unhappy state of the Cornish mines was temporarily forgotten when war came a few months later in August 1914. Jack Holman and the 4th Royal Irish Dragoon Guards were soon sent to France, where the regiment was credited with the first action by the British army in the war. They saw considerable fighting during the first few months and, like many young Cornish soldiers, Jack wrote home and on 21st Sept 1914 the 'Cornish Post & Mining News' published '*another cheery letter from Lieutenant Holman*', written while his regiment, dismounted to serve as infantry, were resting '*after being heavily engaged yesterday. We relieved the infantry and were under heavy fire for some time. We were mentioned in despatches and our major has been recommended for his VC. He is an absolutely topping leader without any fear. For the last two or three days I have not felt very well as I caught a chill from getting soaking wet and then sleeping in my wet clothes. By the way the report of the Germans treatment of our wounded and prisoners are exaggerated colossally.. In fact they fight fairly though there are cases of brutality but there are rotters in every army*'.

Just eight days later Jack Holman was shot through the head by a sniper while trying to rescue a brother officer in the trenches near Armentiers. He endured the long trip back to the field hospital by truck and was taken by train to the main military hospital at Boulogne, meeting an unnamed old school friend on the way. He never recovered and died of his wounds on 30th October 1914. One particularly tragic episode was that his sister went across to nurse him, or at least she believed she was nursing her brother. However, his head was heavily swathed in bandages and it was not discovered until after his death that the army had made a dreadful mistake, for the wounded man was not Jack but another officer named Holman.

Despite James Miners Holman wanting his nephew to remain at home and run the increasingly busy foundry, Treve was all the more determined by his brother's death to join the army. He enlisted in the Royal Field Artillery but he was

Ben Cock, the celebrated manager of No.3 surrounded by one of the three shifts of 'Shell Girls', in 1918. when over two hundred of them were employed by Holmans.

Lunch hour for the 'Shell Girls' in the canteen that was specially provided for them

Holmans had accumulated years of expertise in building small steam engines and easily adapted their production lines to making vertical triple expansion marine engines for the French Navy.

not destined to go to France, where his brother Kenneth and cousin Percy were in the Artillery. Instead he was posted to Mesopotamia. However, he still longed to fly and later transferred to the Hon. Artillery Company, then a training cadre for officers. By early 1918 he was in the Royal Flying Corps and got his wings in June, two months after it became the R.A.F. He was disappointed not to have his wings from the old R.F.C., but was happily transferred to No. 54 Squadron in France. He spent the remainder of the war flying the famous Sopwith '*Camels*'; on ground attack or often low-level missions when the circling SE.5.s and '*Brifits*' drove the '*Huns*' down to the waiting '*Camels*'. Treve never lost his love of flying and years later, even when travelling the world as a successful businessman, he invariably managed to visit the flight deck of the airliner.

Meanwhile Holmans, along with every other Cornish engineering works, had been requisitioned by the government and production lines were reorganised and retooled for war. Ordinary work, except for rock drills for the South African gold mines, virtually ceased. Where mining machinery had once occupied the benches and shop floors, there now appeared a variety of munitions; bomb gauges, powder moulds, tripods for Vickers machine guns, howitzer base plates, paraffin engines and tracks for the amazing new 'Tanks'. One closely overseen section manufactured H.E. Shells and No. 2 works was filled with trawler pattern diesel engines to equip submarine chasers for the French navy. Presses and machinery were also supplied to Bickford Smiths and the National Explosives Co., both heavily engaged in making munitions.

Managing such a complex and often fraught industrial operation rested almost entirely upon James Miners Holman and his nephew Leonard, who, with deep reluctance, had been forced to stay behind while his brothers and cousins served in France. 'Mr Leonard' always regarded his part in the war as '*Inglorious*', yet he was absolutely vital to what had become a busy armaments

Holmans also produced 50 H.P. - 4 cylinder paraffin engines which were fitted into submarine chasers for the British Navy.

Not only did Holmans engine anti-submarine vessels but also made the depth charge throwers that equipped them for their task as here in 1917, each carrying the Royal Seal and a serial number.

used to deputise for his older brothers who worked in the smith's shop, until he became an apprentice in August 1912. After working a hammer and driving the overhead electric crane, he volunteered in 1916, hoping to realise his great ambition of becoming a Guardsman. Instead, he served with the Devons until severely injured at the Battle of Cambrai in September 1918. Many of course never returned to their workbenches. In one edition alone of the 'Cornishman' in August 1918, there were obituaries for two Holman's men; W.C.Trewin who was killed in Flanders after serving in Italy and Lt Cyril Harvey, an ex Holman apprentice who had joined the R.A.F. and was posted missing.

By early in 1915 there was a very serious shortage of manpower throughout the Cornish industries. Old hands due to retire stayed on and others came back. Jebus Bickle, the Cornish engineer, happily came out of retirement to work in the Holman drawing office. James Miners Holman admitted later that, '*the contribution to*

works. However, this did not save him from having a '*White Feather*' thrust into his hands, a cruel and ignorant gesture typical of the times, when people still failed to appreciate that allowing skilled men and managers to enlist might cripple the very industries needed to prosecute the war.

Many had already volunteered or gone with the Territorials and 126 Holman's men would serve in the forces, five of them being commissioned. Private Johns from Tehidy Rd. was among the anti-aircraft gunners who shot down '*L.15*', the first Zeppelin to fall in Britain. The young man who daily drove the pony trap for the manager of Boiler Works soon found himself with the Royal Engineers in Flanders where he served until '*Gassed*' in 1917. Albert Bray, who began as a junior clerk in the head office, joined the D.C.L.I. and swapped cold Camborne for the heat of India. James Mehennet, the son of a manager in the Mysore Goldfields, had become an apprentice in February 1911. He had graduated to the drawing office when he volunteered for the Royal Navy, and was onboard H.M.S. '*Lion*' as an E.R.A. during the Battle of Jutland in May 1916. Thomas Garfield Pidwell, who lived opposite the works,

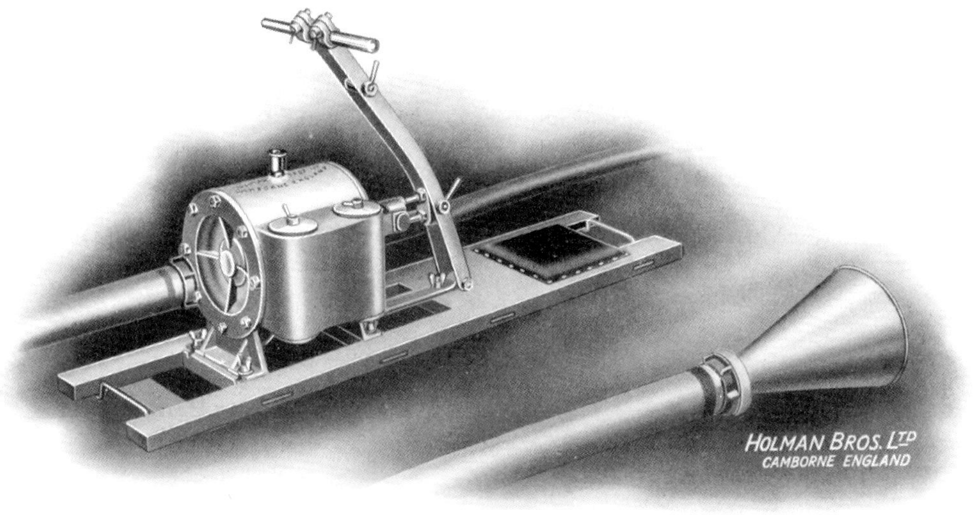

The Holman - Farrar Trench pump was widely used in France to pump out flooded trenches, and being made of aluminium was easily handled and patent valves made it nearly noiseless.

the Empires fighting forces has greatly depleted our workshops of men. Many who formerly stood at the lathes and benches are today in the fighting "Zones" on land or sea in the great conflict.'

The arrival of conscription further depleted manpower and the only solution was the wholesale recruitment of girls and young women. This revived a tradition of women workers in Cornish industry that had ended when the last '*Bal maidens*' left East Pool a few years before. Ben Cock at No.3 rock drill works rapidly found himself managing over 200, which perhaps accounts for the look of slightly sardonic resignation on his face when photographed amid his young ladies. Their immediate foreman was ex-Tuckingmill Foundry apprentice James Parnall, who also belonged to the celebrated Holman Minstrel Troupe and the Holman Quartet that regularly appeared at benefit concerts for good causes or supporting the war effort.
Many girls found that, though long and arduous, war work was an exciting and liberating alternative to the drudgery and poor pay of domestic service or farm work. They excelled as machinists on lathes, shapers and grinders and readily acquired the exacting skills demanded by having to inspect the assembly of intricate components like gauges or gun sights. The more robust even tested the new light jackhammer drills before these were sent to South Africa. All kinds of girls went into munitions, including the author's mother. She was barely seventeen when she found herself assembling shell fuses in the big wooden-hutted works set up on Camborne cricket ground by James Holman's old friend Captain Bennetts of the Roskear Fuse factory. A tribute to the Holman girls came in the company's calendar for 1917. This showed a '*charming young girl in khaki trying out a part of a Holman rock drill, while the Union Jack forms an effective and patriotic background.' 'Carry On' is the title in the footnote. 'Not withstanding the war, production of Holman rock drills is steadily carried on.*' Neither was the birthday of James Miners Holman forgotten when he received a presentation signed by his staff and the heads of departments.

Things were getting more difficult with shortages of food, materials and manpower, as men were being conscripted. Supplying machinery to the Cornish mines was near impossible, let alone to the new mining companies which were ransacking every long forgotten seam for the vital wolfram. Captain Josiah Paull, who was endeavouring to restart Castle and Dinas mine, desperately needed a sand table, which required a priority certificate to enable Holman interrupt their production line. They did ' *promise to proceed with the construction of the table as soon as they have the order, even without a certificate but much prefer to have the latter in case of a munitions inspector calling and possibly stopping the work for something which he would consider more important'*.

War production continued apace with special orders for the 'Wombat' hand-powered drilling machine and the Holman tunnelling pump, both of which were used during tunnel warfare on the Western Front. They were hand worked and relatively silent so as not to reveal the position of the Tunnelling Companies, many manned by Cornish miners, who burrowed deep under the German lines to lay enormous charges of high explosive prior to an offensive.

The hand operated 'Wombat' boring machine was used by the Army Tunnelling Companies in France for a variety of purposes, including mining deep under enemy lines to bury huge explosive charges which would be detonated prior to an offensive.

Many men, like Jack Holman, wrote home about their experiences during the war, but few could rival the extraordinary tale of Arthur Thomas, a first cousin of the Thomas'es of Dolcoath. After managing the El Oro Mine in Mexico and a

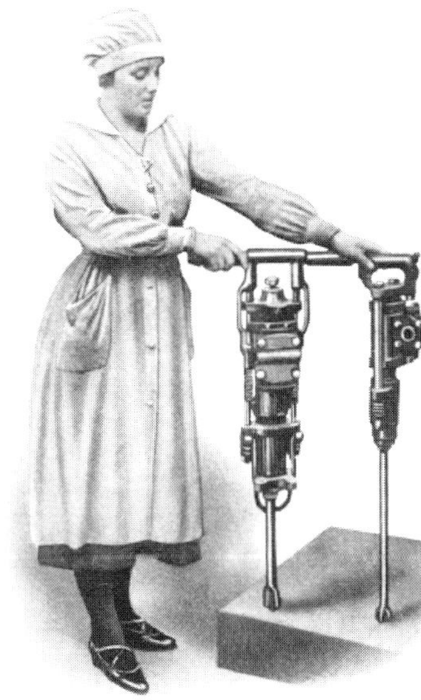

copper mine in Argentina, he went off to Russia as a representative for Holmans, who had a large shareholding in a Siberian Mining Co. By July 1918 he was in Yehkatrenberg which was full of Bolshevik partisans and, as Honorary British Consul, he happily stored the valuables of fellow expatriates and many of the '*White*' Russians, risking being shot if this was discovered. The deposed Czar and his family lived out of sight behind a tall palisade in a small villa, but as the 'Czech Legion' and the 'White' Russian army advanced, Arthur Thomas and everybody else realised that something sinister had happened to the Czar and his family. He was among those invited to inspect the basement of the villa where he was horrified to see blood splashes, fragments of burned clothing and jewellery and the walls pockmarked by bullets, later being told that the bodies had been flung down a derelict mine shaft.

Arthur Thomas left Yehkatrenberg as the Bolsheviks again advanced and on arriving home, related his experiences to Herbert Thomas, the editor of the 'Cornishman'. Herbert, never able to resist a '*scoop*', printed the story of the Czar's execution. This was reprinted in the 'Pall Mall Gazette', mainly because the editor was a Cornishman but it was ignored by the national newspapers who did not carry the story until several months later.

Water Wheels

Overshot and Undershot Wrot Iron and Wood Water Wheels.

Water Wheels are too well known to need any lengthy description. The above illustration shows an overshot Water Wheel. We supply them made of iron throughout, or with wood arms and shrouding. The most satisfactory however, for larger sizes, are those we supply in iron. They are made in all diameters, from 5 to 50 feet, and from 12 inches to 8 feet wide. By forwarding height of fall and approximate quantity of water, we will send size of wheel required.

PRICES AND PARTICULARS ON APPLICATION.

Holman Bros. always had a great tradition of attending exhibitions all over the world and their display at the Wembley Exhibition of May 1924 was one of the most impressive ever staged, engaging the attention of the Prince of Wales and the Royal party.

Chapter Six

Recovery and revival

'*Tourists and others passing through the town of Camborne by rail or road usually express astonishment at discovering a large engineering works in this part of the country. Their astonishment is considerably increased when they stop to investigate and make a tour the various shops of the four sections of the works...*'

Within weeks of the Armistice the lucrative war contracts had been precipitately cancelled without any opportunity for companies to readjust to peace time work. Holmans speedily informed the 'Mining Journal' that they were '*now in a position to receive orders for general machinery*'. Life at the foundry slowly returned to normal, though work now started at 8.am. after the half an hour for breakfast was abolished. A cricket club and tennis club were formed, the rugby team beat St.Ives while Ben cock's artistic nephew, Garstain Cox, having returned from war work had a painting accepted by the RA and was soon being commissioned by Holmans for more calendars.

In reality Holmans quickly discovered that sacrificing normal business for war had a bitter dividend with most of their overseas markets hijacked by the American mining and rock drill companies. The companies only lifeline was new products and hard work by both employees and directors but the same did not apply to the Cornish mines that were once their good customers. Basset Mines collapsed on Christmas Eve 1918, though Major Frank Oats would not see his great mine dismantled as he had died at his daughters house in Port Elizabeth in Natal a few months before. Only the Holman air compressor and the winder survived, the latter going up to a Somerset coalfield where a Holmans man saw it at work many years later.

Even the great Dolcoath was tottering though James Miners Holman, like R. Arthur Thomas was deeply reluctant to see the '*Queen of the*

A Holman 'Jumper' Drill rig, awaiting shipment at No. 1 works in 1924

Cornish Mines' go under. There was little they could achieve, except await the outcome of a deputation to try and secure aid from a government that had more enthusiasm for profitable coal than uneconomic tin. James Holman was still chairman of East Pool whose wartime profits from tin and wolfram enabled the mine to embark on the kind of development denied to Dolcoath. It was believed that the very rich Roger's Lode, discovered in 1915, ran northwards under the old Tolgus Mines, which had never sunk deep enough to strike the tin. Holman and his fellow directors soon formed the Tolgus Tunnel Co. and in February 1919 four Holman 3 $^{1}/_{2}$ inch drifters, mounted side by side in a battery, commenced driving a 10 ft by 8 ft heading 2000 feet northwards from the 255 in Old Agar engine shaft. The urgency of the work was reminiscent of Brakpan or Van Ryn Deep; miners worked continuous six hour shifts and to save time '*mucking out*' after an end was blasted, the broken rock was allowed to fall into a steel net which was hauled clear by a Holman air winch and dumped into empty stopes. A double tram road was installed and a smiths shop and rock drill repair shop cut out of the solid rock.

Driving through increasingly hard granite, the tunnel at 860 feet cut through a very rich lode of tin and wolfram then came disaster. Early in May 1922 there were small roof falls in the Great Gunnis at the 180 in East Pool; these increased and became a huge subterranean landslide as the old copper workings collapsed downwards. Shafts were blocked, including North Whim which was worked by the Holman beam winder, and worse all pumping ceased. The flooding threatened South Crofty while down in the Tolgus Tunnel, 1600 feet under Illogan Churchyard, the Holman crews faced an inrush of 25 gallons per minute.

East Pool appeared doomed to become just another '*knackt bal*' but James Holman and his directors reacted with a swiftness rare in Cornish mining. To regain Roger's Lode they would shift the mine to the opposite of the main road and on

The busy machine shop & erection shop at No. 1 around 1924.

A quarryman using a Holman jackhammer perched high on the ledges of North Wales slate quarry in 1932.

Amy Johnson, the celebrated lady aviator 'working' a Holman PV. drifter at the bottom of an Australian Mine in 1932.

21 October 1921 they commenced sinking the new Taylor's Shaft, which in 20 months was due to bottom out at 250 fathoms. East Pool used their own miners and the new Holman HD.3. Hammer drills, which, to the delight of Captain Taylor, easily put down 20 foot holes in the hardest greenstone and would have done double that if required, a response that soon appeared in Holmans publicity.

The fortunes of East Pool contrasted sharply with the rest of the '*Black Country*' around Camborne for, even as the Holman drills bored steadily downwards, the depression had worsened. Carn Brea Mine had finally closed in January 1921 and Captain Josiah Paull had reluctantly put South Crofty into care and maintenance Things were so bad the Cornish Electric Power Co. deprived of many good customers, was uncertain about supplying the surviving mines or even the Holman foundry and the tram cars running between Camborne and Redruth. The Holman's men themselves willingly donated to the relief fund for the unemployed miners while the Holman Male Voice Choir would soon embark on a tour to raise money for the same fund. Later John Holman himself had to lay off men from throughout the works until orders revived.

The catastrophic collapse of East Pool did provide some extra work as threatened by serious flooding, Captain Paull of South Crofty promptly wired the liquidator of Grenville Mine not to sell the 90 inch pumping engine on Fortescue's shaft. Privately he reckoned '*it would be worth while to secure the plant if only on spec as the sum I have valued it at is practically breaking up price*'. Holmans were now the only foundry capable of making the pitwork and heavy castings required for a Cornish pumping engine. On 18th March 1922 Captain Paull wrote '*... I told Holman Bros. yesterday to get on with the pitwork anyway. They hope to deliver the set for the 195 in 4 or 5 weeks and the other sets as we want them at 1 or 2 week intervals*'.

Captain Paull's bargain buys, including two steel Lancashire boilers, whose price he had managed to '*whittle down*' arrived behind a pair of traction engines in May 1922. The installation of the 'Ninety' and the new engine house of shuttered concrete was supervised by Joe Blight, an ex 'Climax' apprentice who had worked on the

A Geevor miner using a Holman cradle drifter, mounted on a 'Bar and Arm' 1934

installation of the Severn Tunnel Pumps but it was a laborious task. By early August Captain Paull was able to report that the *'biggest items of the engine viz. the bob and the cylinder are in position'* though it was October before the Holman pitwork was in position. There were other delays until on 20 November 1922 Captain Paull recorded that *'We only ran the engine about half an hour yesterday afternoon to see if everything was all right and I am pleased to say both engine and pitwork was as near perfect as one could wish, no leakage of steam anywhere and in the shaft the pitwork was very steady'.*

Alfred Angove, who became a Holman apprentice in January 1896, using a chipping hammer on the cast iron centre for a large dipper wheel in the foundry in 1924

James Holmans steadfast dedication to Cornish mining was demonstrated only a few months later when undismayed by the loss of the Tolgus Tunnel, the East Pool committee decided to sink a shaft right where it should have ended. The Tolgus Shaft Co., was formed and in May 1922 Holman drills began sinking a 17ft by 8 ft shaft among the old Tolgus mines. By December the shaft was down 500 feet and was to sink another 1500 before cross cutting out to the S.W. but it was one of the biggest and most expensive failures in Cornish mining.

At Dolcoath the drive under the Roskears had not been abandoned, even when the mine finally shut down in April 1921. A new company was formed with Holman and his son, Leonard, among the directors and early in 1923 R Arthur Thomas announced that New Dolcoath would be sunk in the heart of the Roskears. Piggotts the Welsh pit sinkers, who had put down Williams Shaft a decade before contracted to sink the new shaft, which was slightly smaller than the latter though also brick lined.

By July 1924 the new shaft was down to 400 feet and R. Arthur Thomas was determined that he would not have some redundant 'Eighty' or 'Ninety' erected on his modern mine, even *'if the Cornish engine persists in its reputation as evidenced by the attitudes of the management of South Crofty and East Pool'*. The electric pumps were raised from Willaims shaft, which was stripped of its machinery but the amazing Holman winder was too unique to be re-used.

The steam winder from Harriet Shaft, though elderly was used, being rebuilt and given an overwind trip and speeded up to hoist at 2000 feet per minute. Holmans engineers dismantled the cross compound air compressor at Williams shaft and later the big lattice head gear which was tailored to fit Roskear Shaft as a replacement for that from Harriet that was used as temporary sinking head frame.

James Holmans unremitting faith in Cornish mining was never really rewarded as both the Tolgus tunnel and New Dolcoath were expensive failures. His sons and nephews were convinced that the future of Holman Brothers lay in developing new products and customers and the pursuit of foreign orders was to remain the almost sacred duty of the directors for generations to come. More immediately the task was to regain those customers lost through the concentration upon war work and the Holman boys resumed their frenetic sales trips all over the world. Treve Holman had barely returned home from flying 'Camels' in Flanders, when, after pausing to get married and abandoning the opportunity to stand for Parliament, he sailed for South Africa, together with Ben Cock, just as W C Stephens returned after a successful trip to the Witerwatersrand. Treve was to make frequent visits to the gold mines and once returned with a painful souvenir as, when laughing over some joke in a stope, he was struck in the teeth by a flying pebble.

American companies now monopolised the gold mines though Holman 3 ½ Drills had established another record by sinking the main shaft at

The powerful and versatile Holman air winch was widely used all over the mining world as here in a South African gold mine stope around 1933.

Crown Deep in July 1919; 4 drifters and 2 jackhammers sank the the South African equivielnt of Willam's Shaft 279 feet in 31 days and then followed up with a stoping record at Van Ryn Deep. The Holman Agency was still managed by C.F.E. Vivian, who, after mining in East pool and on the Rand, had joined them in 1911. There were then only three employees, supervised by J.H.Vivian and the agency operated as a department of Fraser Chalmers Ltd.

Mr Percy after a trip to India, came out to the Rand himself early in 1922 and spent a year in Johannesburg organising the business. By 1927 Holman South Africa (Proprietary) Ltd had been established and developed into a large engineering works capable of supplying machinery and spare parts. Mr Leonard went off to Canada and returned home in time to leave for Spain with Mr Kenneth who had been made a director in August 1922. The important West African goldfields were not neglected and by 1933 a branch had been established at Takoradi where work shops, staff bungalows and 'Cornwall' House had been built to house staff servicing Nigeria, Sierra Leone, the Cameroons and the Gold Coast.

A new development were the 'S.L' or 'Stream Lined' drills when, to eliminate projections like the valve chest, the valves were placed at the rear of the machine, ensuring quicker action for less air. New circular valves replaced the tappets and steel balls and 'kicker ports' were introduced to speed up the valve action and increase drilling speed. The air winches were also developed into newer models, the largest capable of hoisting a ton vertically, or double that up a 30 degree slope. The stretcher bar hoists had come far since the days of James Holman's shipboard chat with the homeward bound mining engineers; the most powerful could raise a ton and a half, or drag 3 tons up a very steep incline. One innovation was the Heal - Shaw Beecham air motor which was capable or working even under water, and was fitted to a range of Holman equipment including the 'Superhaul'. where it was mounted inside the winding drum. Much of the new equipment was displayed at the British Empire Exhibition held at Wembley Exhibition in the May of 1924. The

Every rock drill made by Holmans was tested at the 'Test Mine', a small granite quarry at Carwinnen near Troon, which was acquired by the company in 1920. Trials of prototypes and modified machines and training of the noble art of rock drilling was also carried out in the mine, which probably contains more holes per square foot than any other rock face in the world.

Prince of Wales and the Duke and Duchess of York spent considerable time at the impressive Holman's exhibition stand and the company subsequently produced a magnificent souvenir brochure which was the first ever pictorial record of the whole works.

Holman guaranteed that every piece of equipment was thoroughly tested before leaving the works and to ensure this in 1920 they acquired a small granite quarry near Blackrock at Troon. Hundreds of rock drills were tried out in what always became known as the 'Test Mine' and a notebook, written in faded pencil there such entries as *'Jan 1926 Tested new 50 lb. Light Drifter with vent washer. Will not stand any strain all air blowing through vent holes' or '24 Jan. Light Drifter came back from Cumberland tendency to stop when pressure put on it. Valve has not enough air to blow it over when back'.* The writer was Richard 'Dick' Gilbert who at thirteen had been apprenticed to Harvey of Hayle and that foundry closed had with another young man demolished a 135 foot chimney. He joined Holmans as a fitter in 1904 at No 1. but the next year migrated to the USA. and on returning in

Ben Keast of St. Just using a small Holman hammer drill in Geevor around 1935

1907 went to the Rock Drill shop at No.3. One of his earliest jobs was to go up to Milliom in Cumberland and install new condencer work and pipes on a 70 inch engine but he soon displayed an absolute genius for rock drill development and

Holmans always had many customers in India and here a portable compressor, shielded from the blistering sun by a makeshift awning, is being used on what appears to be a mining prospect near Hyderabad in 1933.

In 1930 the Holman repair shops in Johannesburg are far removed from the cramped tin sheds at the beginning of the century. This shop and two others were well equipped and operated and evolved into a large plant producing machines and spare parts.

Camborne roadmen dig their way up Beacon Hill with SS.23 Road Rippers fed by a portable compressor around 1932.

he and Mr Treve were largely responsible for opening the Test Mine.

By January 1924 the 'Mining World' reported that the '*famous mine engineering works - of Messrs Holman at Camborne, there is work in abundance even to the extent of entailing overtime employment in some departments*'. There were now 532 employees and, unlike many Cornish firms, Holmans had taken on fifteen disabled servicemen and were ready to employ more to fill their government quota. This was typical of the Holman boys who saw their civic responsibilities as inseparable from their own business. To promote the skills and prospects of their apprentices they were given the opportunity to sit the exams which brought prize money, diplomas and free evening classes at the Mining school. One of the earliest scholars was George Lawry, the son of Sergeant Major Lawry, who had joined No 1. stores in 1912 and after service in France returned to operate the head office telephone exchange. His other two other sons, both apprentices, were already working in the USA.

When fourteen year old Harry Blackwell signed his indentures on 8 August 1932, they were no longer printed in elegant script but still signed by James Miners Holman himself. Young Blackwell already had a rich Cornish engineering background as his grandfather had installed Holman boilers in India, and his father, after serving an apprenticeship at Cox & Co. of Falmouth, had gone out to the Witwatersrand. There was joined his brother, '*Uncle Charlie Blackwell*', an ex Harvey apprentice who, having relinquished his job at the London Waterworks, arrived at his parents door to inform them he was off to South Africa and, turning about caught the next train for London. He became chief engineer at Ferreira Deep and as a celebrated racing car enthusiast, won the M.C. by leading a motorised column into German South West Africa in 1914.

Young Harry whose later career was more adventurous than his uncles, was a reluctant apprentice, more so when his weekly wage rose to 4/- and then 1/2d. was deducted for insurance. His father remained adamant that he should stay

Holman 'Road Ripper' at work in London Street around 1930

as a '*Holman indenture was worth its weight in gold all over the world*'. The hours were long 8.30 am to 5.30 p.m. with Saturday morning working. Half an hour was allowed for cleaning down the benches, which was often accompanied to the singing of men, who belonged to the Holman Male Voice Choir.

John Miners Holman, now nearing seventy remained outwardly the *'Presiding genius'* at Holmans and was still '*a gentleman largely esteemed by all who knew him at home or overseas and greatly loved by the staff he employs*'. The grand old man of Cornish engineering received the ultimate accolade when the Prince of Wales visited the foundry on 20th May 1926. The prince and the Duke of York had spent some time at the company's stand at Wembley when he expressed a desire to visit the works but, his arrival was so sudden that Holmans were almost taken by surprise. Resplendent in plus fours and a fuschia coloured tie and accompanied by Sir Walter Peackcock, Secretary of the Duchy, the prince jumped smartly out of his car at 3pm outside to No 1. though the suddenness of his visit meant that there was only a small crowd. He was greeted by Treve, Percy, Leonard and Nicholas Curry and, after asking to be introduced to each foreman, was escorted into the moulding shop where he saw a chipping hammer and a patent moulding sand rammer at work. In the pattern shop he met the oldest employee, William Harris who had been with Holmans since 1901. He spoke with Sydney Nettle who had joined the company in 1895 and in the smiths shop met the venerable John Veale who, now seventy had begun as an apprentice with John Holman back in 1868 and whose own father had worked in the old foundry. He was not the only old hand as in No.1 erection shop the prince shook hands with the foreman Harry Harvey, congratulating him on forty five years service before being shown an air compressor fly wheel being turned and a boring mill at work. Although the prince's tour was still being conducted at a 'smart pace' he paused in the yard next to Dolcoath Road to inspect two of Holman's increasingly popular portable air compressors, one driven by petrol and the other by diesel.

Half an hour later the Prince was on his way to No.3 where, news having spread of the visit, so large a crowd had gathered that the police had to control the traffic. He was greeted at the main entrance by Ben Cock, the manager and his brother William and as no special arrangements had been made he met the men as if it was an ordinary working day. His interest was genuine and thorough as he progressed through each department until well over time he paused before leaving at the main entrance to watch Dick Gilbert, bore 17 inches in hard granite in a minute with a stoping drill.

A petrol driven portable compressor at work at Reichenback, Germany in 1934

The portable compressors so proudly shown to the Prince of Wales belonged to a new generation of vertical high speed machines that had superseded the great engineering battleships installed at Dolcoath and Levant. Above all they were mobile; just as Trevithick had put wheels on his '*Puffer*' engines and created road and rail locomotives, so Holmans had put wheels on their new powerful air compressors, and opened a new era for civil engineering and themselves. New drills were needed and so arrived the '*Road Breaker*' and the '*Road Ripper*' which in the fists of large and lusty road men would often destroy the peace of leafy suburbia for the next seventy years.

By the 1930s the 'Type 'T'' double stage differential piston compressor had been introduced and with various modifications and developments remained the standard model until the 1960s. All this sophistication still relied on robust testing and the compressors were regularly towed at speed along the cliff by Holmans new Thorneycroft Lorry which had replaced horses in 1926. On a memorable occasion one of the spoked *'artillery'* wheels came off, and breaking tow, the compressor slewed to a stop on the edge of Hells Mouth. The new compressors found ready markets including the naval dockyards and were also used to help salvage the sunken German battle ships in Scapa Flow. In 1929 the Holman compressor won a Silver Medal and Diploma at the Royal Cornwall Polytechnic Society's exhibition, just fifty years after the 'Cornish' Rock Drill was given its maiden trial by the same Cornish body.

It was at this time that Holmans embarked on the design and development of pneumatic tools and created another product that became synonomous with their name. Air tools had been in use for a long time and, like the rock drill, owed much to American inventive genius. By 1896 the superintendent of the Union Pacific Railroad's locomotive works at Omaha, claimed that in his machine shops '*air was as important as steam*' while Naval dockyard and the G.W.R. workshops at Swindon already relied heavily on imported American air tools.

The Prince of Wales using a test gauge during his visit

The development of the 'vane' type air motor made possible the application to an even wider variety of tools, and potential did not escape the Holman boys who had gained considerable experience of small machine and component manufacture through their war work. In 1919 Ben Cock had designed a

A Holman Air winch and air compressor perched on an impossibly frail staging set up in the river near Chittagong in Jan 1930.

concrete breaker based on the air valve drill and by the early 1920s an experimental 'P.T.' shop was established at No.3.

There was a brief co-operation with 'F.T.A.C.' an Italian compressed air company but pnuematic tool development increased significantly when in August 1924 Holmans employed J.H.Arthur who already held several patents and had worked for Armstrong Whitworth and the British Pnuematic Tool Co. at Coventry. Soon there was a production line turning out chippers, riveting and caulking hammers and the very successful coal pick which was used in thousands in the Welsh mines.

By 1930 it had '*become 'imperitive to find a new home' for the 'P.T.' shops'* which was quickly transferred to the old Public Rooms adjacent to No.3. and further expanded with new tooling, just as the '*Great Depression*' struck Camborne. 'P.T.' barely managed to survive but production was eventually restored and, a new range of air tools and machinery were exhibited at the British Industries Fair in April 1932. These included a special core drill, developed for the Ministry of Transport, to check whether the concrete used in making new roads had been perfectly laid. The 1936 Catalogue reflected the increasing importance of pnuematic tools, besides the innovation of '*Hot Mill'* drill bit sharpening and the 'Vee' engines, thousands of which were in use in the Welsh collieries.

Although his health was failing James Miners Holman would live to see one his most cherished ambitions come to fruition. Always aware of his grandfathers friendship with Richard Trevithick and his family's roots in the industrial revolution he was determined to have a fitting memorial to the great engineer in his home town. In 1911 he with C.V.Thomas and J.J.Beringer, the principal of Camborne School of Mines established the Trevithick Memorial Committee. By 1914 they had raised £600 when it was decided to increase the height of the proposed bronze statue an extra foot to 7 foot 6 inches which brought the bill to £1,000. The outbreak of war saw the quest laid aside but in 1917 a model statue was made and

Holman employees in 1936

displayed at the Royal Academy, though there was no opportunity to make castings until peace came. The first memorial was a plaque commemorating the maiden trial of the Road Locomotive and set into the stone wall around Roswarne at the bottom of Tehidy Road being unveiled during the Peace Day Celebrations on 19 July 1919.

James Miners Holman had also proposed that the memorial should also include a '*Trevithick Scholarship*' at the Camborne School of Mines and, during his visit to South Africa in 1922 raised £200 for the project. Eventually the whole memorial was '*completed mainly through the generous gifts and personal efforts of J.M.Holman*'.

The statue of Richard Trevithick was offically unveiled in a memorable ceremony by the Duke of Kent on 17 May 1932. The Duke had landed in his aircraft at Tehidy and at lunch at Camborne School of Mines was introduced to the memorial committee including Leonard and Treve Holman, who represented their father. Early in the afternoon they escorted him around the works and then came the ceremony itself with a crowd of thousands surrounding Camborne Public Library where the bronze Richard Trevithick stood on a pedestal of Cornish granite. There was a guard of honour from the British Legion. and the Duke also inspected the Boy Scouts, and Girls Guides to the cheering of 2,000 children lining his route. C.V. Thomas spoke at length on Trevithick and also the unstinting dedication of James Miners Holman in ensuring that the great Cornish engineer had a fitting memorial he then invited Leonard Holman, on behalf of his father to ask the Duke to unveil the statue.

James Miners Holman died at Rosewarne on the evening of Monday 28 February 1933. For over fifty years he had been '*A Camborne Captain of Industry*' whose career embraced the advent of the rock drill and the development of Holman Brothers as a world wide company. His funeral cortege was headed by his sons and nephews and the Holman's men, while flags hung at half mast above the works which had been closed for the day. Yet his was not only the funeral in Camborne that day as by tragic coincidence Garstain Cox had died the evening after James Holman. He had been unwell for some time but had come over from his home on the Lizard to nurse his father and caught influenza which became pnuemonia. He was only forty one with much of his artistic career still before him, and his talent was recognised by Stanhope Forbes and by his old teacher Lamorna Birch. His funeral at Roskear Church was as large as James Holman, and attended by Ben Cock and his other uncles, C.V. Thomas and Mr Warren from Boiler Works while the bearers included Dick Gilbert and Percy Tromans.

It was about this time the Levant Mine finally closed down and those miners still left, began breaking the big collection of machinery at surface. The old Harvey pumping engine was speedily dismantled, though the bob fell and becoming wedged fast had to be blown up inside the house. A start was made on the Harvey winding engine, that for ninety years had hoisted from 'Skip Shaft', but for virtually the first time came the realisation that such a uniquely historic engine should be saved for posterity. The cause was taken up by Cornish scholar Tregonning Hooper and Jack Trounson of Redruth, whose knowledge and enthusiasm for the Cornish engine was unrivalled at a time when 'Industrial Archaeology' was still forty years in the future. They approached Treve Holman, who was himself deeply concerned and well aware that Cornwall's industrial heritage was being swept away. With his enthusiastic help and support they formed the Cornish Engines Preservation Society in 1935. The Levant engine was restored and the house made weather tight while the public was admitted right up to the outbreak of war, though these early pioneers of 'Industrial archaeology' could not have guessed that sixty years later the Levant engine would once more be steaming on the St.Just cliffs.

"Holman" Diagonal Hoist with Vertical Boiler.

Chapter Seven

War again

'The dreaded Holman projector'

The war was only a fortnight old when the restless and inventive mind of Treve Holman evolved a way of converting compressed air into an offensive weapon. With his wide knowledge of technical history he knew the idea was not new; the ancient Greeks had first fired arrows with compressed air. The famous charge of Teddy Roosevelt's *'Rough Riders'* at San Juan during the Spanish American war of 1898 was supported by a Simms Dudley compressed air cannon firing shells packed with Nobel blasting explosives. The U.S. Navy had tried a battery of compressed air guns on the USS 'Vesuvias' while the Brazilians tested a large naval gun charged by a three-stage compressor. The first ever 'Whitehead' torpedo was also propelled by compressed air.

Treve Holman, like Cousin Percy, easily recalled the Stokes mortar which was widely used in the trenches in Flanders, and he was convinced that compressed air was as good a propellant as cordite. In typical fashion, a prototype was hurriedly built from material lying around No. 1.

Richard 'Dick' Gilbert, O.B.E. who, with Treve Holman, worked on the development of the Holman Projector, and seen here 'Loading' a Mk.3. in the Holman workshops late in 1941.

It was quite simple, with a steel tube welded to an air tank and fitted with a quick release valve, which was triggered by the missile. During tests, a heavy weight was fired over twenty feet and, after further modifications, the mortar blew a heavier missile even higher.

Thus, by the autumn of 1939, the 'Holman Projector' had been born; one of the most unorthodox yet successful A.A. weapons of World War Two. Also, strikingly, it was not the creation of a group of '*Boffins*' or some sophisticated armament works but came from a relatively small works in the far west of Cornwall. Treve Holman still faced the daunting task of convincing the military, who naturally were always less than enthusiastic about innovative weapons. Fortunately the Holman Projector attracted the attention of Captain John Leach R.N., Director of Naval Ordinance, whose help and advice was to be crucial in the coming months. Commodore Young of the Naval gunnery school on Whale Island at Portsmouth was sent to Camborne to inspect the projector and especially to discover its potential against low flying bombers. During the three days he spent at Holmans, the mounting was redesigned and rebuilt at his suggestions and after more tests another prototype was built. The specification demanded that the projector should be made only from readily available materials such as steel and cast iron and be capable of firing a standard mills bomb with a 3.5 second fuse to 1000 feet, while the receiver must hold sufficient for 50 firings at 30 RPM.

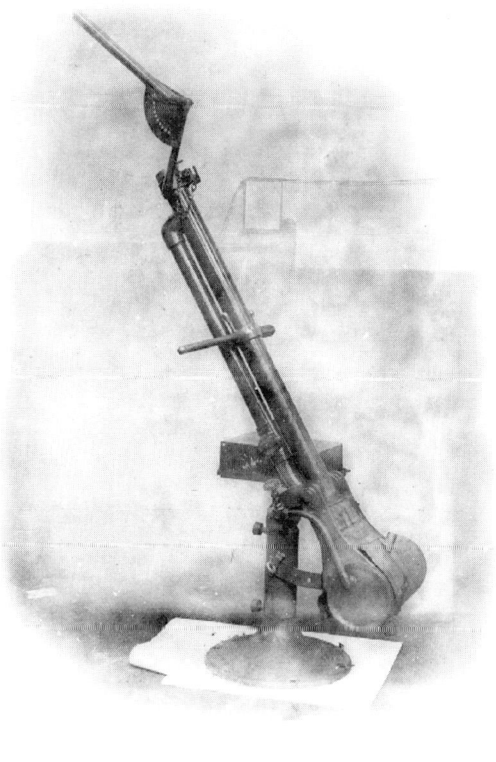

The Mk.1. automatic firing Holman Projector

In February 1940 the projector was tested at Whale Island where Treve Holman and his team found themselves ranged in a line with six other hopeful new weapons, each inventor avidly eyeing the competition. The first live firing tests were a fiasco. Having seen a rival's rocket round vanish towards Portsmouth, the Holman's men loaded and fired but there was only a faint click and hiss of air and the mills bomb dropped only 50 feet away. '*Within two seconds not a soul could be seen. After a short time had elapsed and no explosion had occurred, a head appeared here and another there. Finally a rating crawled over to the bomb and dropped it into a bucket of water*'. The Mills bomb was a dummy and therefore too light to trigger the firing mechanism but loaded with the proper ammunition the projector was highly effective.

Awaiting testing Mk.1. Projectors lined up on the Porthtowan firing range.

There was an unforeseen sequel to the trial when Treve Holman called at the gunnery offices next morning to collect some prints he had forgotten. Stories of German spies were rife and even after being interrogated by Naval officers for ten minutes it still took two hours to get him back.

The trial led to an order for 1000 but this was cut by half by the development of the improved Mk 2 Projector that was capable of firing two Mills Bombs detonating at half- second intervals. Automatic firing was replaced by a simple twist handle, while the bomb canister was redesigned so that the lid fell away after half a second at about 100 feet, releasing the side lever and arming the missile. The straight bar sight was mounted at an angle of 20 degrees below the muzzle and for the first round it was pointed ahead of the target and the '*aim then corrected by observation of the flight of the bombs. Bombs should burst on or ahead of the target as bursts astern will have no moral or material effect*'. Gunners were warned to be careful of the controls and to conserve the air supply especially when '*in a locality in which Attack by Enemy Aircraft is possible*' and to '*Keep air cock on receiver firmly closed until action begins*. One bonus was that on exploding, the bombs left a heavy puff of black smoke which made the German bombers believe they faced heavy '*Flak*' and not merely a simple mortar made down in Camborne.

Coastal ships and patrol boats, even the RMS '*Scillonian*', were fitted with projectors while naval crews and merchant sailors came from as far away as Stornoway to attend courses at Holmans, which included two or three days on the firing range at Porthtowan, where most of the test work was done.

A batch was shipped up to Aberdeen and within weeks came the first confirmed kill, during an attack on the steam coaster '*Highlander*', which, commanded by captain William Gifford, sailed from Abderdeen for Leith on the evening of 1 August 1940. She did not ship Naval gunners but some of her crew had been trained at the D.E.M.S .school to operate her meagre A-A defences, a Holman projector on the foc's'le and an ancient Lewis gun in a sand bagged mounting on the stern.

Treve Holman, though nursing a broken arm, stands by a Mk.1. projector at the Porthtowan firing range.

Anxious regarding the effects of intense heat upon a mills bomb in the Mk.2. steam projector, Treve Holman borrowed a steam roller from Cornwall County Council and 'cooked' the bomb for twenty minutes. Nothing happened and the bomb was then fired a thousand feet into the air.

There was still a faint glimmer of summer dusk when at 11 45 p.m. the '*Highlander*' was attacked 6 miles south of Stone Haven by a pair of Heinkel He.115 Flying boats, slow but sufficiently well armed to hunt the North Sea Convoys. The second mate, seeing the white splash of a torpedo striking the sea, put the helm hard over. The torpedo passed close under the stern and Captain Giffard radioed 'A-A-A-A' signifying air attack

The coastal steamer 'Highlander' lying badly damaged at Leith after her successful battle with two Heinkel Floatplanes, which were shot down by her Lewis guns and Holman Projector in August 1940. This particular projector, riddled with shrapnel and machine gun fire was for many years a prized exhibit in the Holman Museum.

to Cullercoats Radio who alerted the Royal Navy. The Heinkel banked around and came in again, her gunners raking the 'Highlander's' port side. Her own gunners were ready and "*Fire was opened by ship's machine gun and Holman Projector... at 00.10 am. ..Enemy aircraft which was still attacking and low over the vessel, was struck by gunfire from ship and crashed, partly on deck and partly in water in flames. Considerable damage was done to the ship's superstructure rails etc.. lifeboats No 4. and 5 were smashed, Wireless Aerial put out of action, Holman Projector also put out of action and William Birnie AB. and Bert Whyman, Fireman, who were operating the same received facial injuries. The said injured men received first aid on board'.*

Resolutely Captain Giffard resumed his voyage but at '*..00.30 a.m., the vessel was again attacked by enemy aircraft, and two aerial torpedoes were seen in close vicinity which again passed close astern...gunfire was returned from the ship.. until 00.50 am when Aircraft was hit and crashed into the sea about 100 yards astern of ship*".

Battered and smoking the 'Highlander' reached Leith at 10am and so famous was the episode that Muirhead Bone, the eminent war artist was sent to sketch her. When news reached Treve Holman, he had the damaged projector sent back to Camborne where many years later it was proudly displayed in the 'Holman Museum'.

Within a month of the attack on the '*Highlander*' every trawler skipper was clamouring for a Holman Projector to reinforce his Hotchkiss or Lewis Gun. Most of their vessels were steam and Admiral Leach rang Treve Holman asking if the projector could be converted to steam. This was feasible except that Treve Holman was worried about the effect of the heat upon the Mills bomb. A test was arranged at Porthtowan when a steamroller borrowed from Cornwall County

Council was connected up to a projector. The driver duly raised the pressure to 200 P.S.I. and the bomb was '*Cooked*' for twenty minutes without any ill effect and when it next fired a round, it performed perfectly, shooting the bomb over 1,000 feet high.

During the summer of 1940, Sir Winston Churchill himself demanded a demonstration but on arriving at the Aldershot range, Treve Holman and his team found the army had not provided any ammunition. The 'P.M.' was already displaying his notorious impatience when someone recalled that there were bottles of beer in their picnic lunch hamper. The first bottle burst in the barrel but the next landed squarely on target, which provoked Sir Winston to jovially remark that it would '*save on cordite*'.

From the time of introduction the Holman projector slowly began to notch up a tally of German bombers, usually putting up a grenade barrage in support of fire from Hotchkiss or Lewis guns. A list of successful engagements still survives in the Holman archive.

1st June 1940	*SS. ' Bombay'*	1 probable	Holman & Hotchkiss gun.
1st Aug. 1940	*SS.'Highlander'*	2 confirmed	Holman & Lewis gun.
8th Dec. 1940	*SS.'Treverbyn'*	1 damaged	Holman & Hotchkiss gun
26th Jan 1941	*HMS 'Reids'*	1 confirmed	Holman and Lewis.
	HMT 'Lord St.Vincient'	1 confirmed	Holman and Lewis
12th Feb. 1941	*HMT. Eager'*	1 confirmed	Holman & Lewis
27th Feb 1941	*HMT 'Lord Stonehaven'*	1 damaged	Holman, Lewis & 0.5.
13th Mar 1941	*SS.'Instrahull'*	1 damaged	Holman, & machine guns
23rd Mar.1941	*SS.'Beltoy'*	1 probable	12 pdr. Lewis & Holman
6th Mar. 1941	*SS 'Andoni'*	1 damaged	Holman, Lewis & Hotchkiss
18 Mar. 1941	*FT. Thracian' and 'Kingsway'*	1 confirmed	Holman and Lewis
2 April 1941	*HMS.'Silver Dawn'*	1 damaged	Holman, Lewis, 2 pdr.
9 April 1941	*HMT ' Avondale' &*	1 damaged	Holman, Hotchkiss,
	HMT 'Lord Nuffield'		12 pdr and Lewis.
27 April 1941	*HMS 'Patia'*	1 confirmed	Holman, Hotchkiss, 3
			ins. 2 pdr. & Harvey.
27 April 1941	*SS 'Marie Dawn'*	1 confirmed	Hotchkiss, Lewis & Holman
4 May 1941	*M.V. 'Araybank'*	2 confirmed	Holman and Hotchkiss.
18 May 1941	*HMS 'Corinthian'*	1 damaged	Holman, Hotchkiss 12 pdr.
20 June 1941	*SS 'Dalemoor'* and others	1 probable	Holman, Lewis and Hotchkiss
		1 damaged	
28 July 1914	*HMS. 'Typhoon'*	1 confirmed	Holman, 12 pdr. Lewis and
			Hotchkiss
4 Aug 1941	*HMS.'Norland'*	1 confirmed.	Holman, 12 Pdr.Hotchkiss &
			Lewis.
15 July 1942	*HML. ' 141'.*	1 confirmed	0.5. Lewis and Holman
		1 damaged	
	HML. '139'	1 probable	0.5. Lewis and Holman

A training session for troops on the Porthtowan firing range with the Mk.1. Holman projector mounted on a stout wooden wagon early in 1940.

Treve Holman himself received news of one spectacular success for his projector.

" Dear Mr Holman,

Commander Young has given me a piece of very good news to pass onto you and all working on the Projectors.

A Holman Projector has shot down a 4-engined Focke-Wulf in mid - Atlantic. The machine, which was flying very low, was hit at the root of one of the wings and crashed into the water..... "

The Focke-Wulf '*Kondor*' was the very long-range bomber which harassed allied shipping from bases in Brittany and was a deadly opponent, even for a fighter, let alone a ship armed merely with a primitive air mortar. Evidently, with ammunition running low for both Lewis gun and 12 pdr., a gunner had desperately loaded the projector with three mills bombs and caught the '*Kondor*' at close range.

The Holman projector continued to be modified for a variety of roles on both land and sea. Being smooth bore it could fire almost anything from anti-tank rounds to the '*Molotov Cocktail*', the celebrated petrol bomb in a glass bottle. Successful tests were also made firing a Schermuly lifesaving rocket line and projectors were adapted to fire grapnel lines to the tops of cliffs for the benefit of the commandos. Another development was the '*Chough*' gun, a short-barrelled projector using cordite propellant and fitted with a gunshield. The '*Chough*' was capable of firing a wide variety of ordnance, including flares, grenades, spigot mortars and anti - tank rounds.

At the request of captain 'D' at Devonport, the Holman projectors were adapted to fire a 12 lb.

Sir Winston Churchhill, standing beside a Holman Projector waves fairwell to the battleship 'Prince of Wales', the flagship of Admiral Sir John Leach, one of the strongest supporters of the development of the weapon. Such was his enthusiasm that the Admiral had a projector mounted on his barge, but sadly he was lost when the 'Prince of Wales' was sunk by Japanese bombers off Malaya in December 1941.

In 1943 two survivors from a German E-Boat, sunk by British Coastal Forces in the English Channel, stand under guard on the counter of a M.C.B., one apprehensively clutching the training bar of a Holman Projector.

rocket flare especially to take advantage of the weapon's near noiseless and flashless operation. Once at the desired height, the rocket ignited and flew for a mile and a half until the flare itself burst, burning at 600,000 candlepower for 45 seconds. Both the Mk.2's and the Mk 3's were modified for special tasks, some being given a '*By pass barrel*' to vent excess air or cordite gas. This ensured a pre-set accuracy for the projectile, making it ideal for anti - submarine operations. Projectors were sent to Gibraltar to counter the successful raids by Italian frogmen and charioteers against shipping moored in the harbour. Incidentally they were not the only Holman equipment in action on the great fortress, as Holman S.L.9 Rock drills, air compressors and drill sharpeners were then being used to drive galleys and defensive tunnels. Holmans even in wartime achieved a record when an 8 ft by 8ft heading was driven 180 feet in a remarkable 7 days.

The Holman Projector became a truly offensive weapon during the battles between the Naval Coastal Forces and the German E-Boat flotillas in the close waters of the English Channel. It was a war of sudden ambushes and high-speed chases on black nights lit by flares or the quick flash of tracer fire. Not quite the theatre of operations for the sedentary projector but the weapons potential was recognised by Lt-Commander Robert Hitchens R.N.V.R., a peacetime solicitor and international dinghy sailor who lived at Constantine and was also deputy town clerk of Helston. He saw that with only a light recoil and not requiring a heavy mounting, the projector was ideal for the lightly built motor gunboats then attacking the German convoys off the Dutch coast. These were always covered by the heavily armed E-boats and '*Flak*' ships and Lt-Commander Hitchens, operating from Felixstowe under the Nore Command, evolved many tactics for thwarting the enemy. Indeed, he became the supreme tactician for the Coastal Forces. When going into the attack he divided his forces into two sections. One section used their projectors to

The works manager, Nicholas Curry, escorts Queen Elizabeth, the Queen Mother, during the royal visit to Holman Brothers in May 1942.

fire flares above the E-Boats, which confused them as to their attackers' position, thanks to the projectors lack of flash or noise. The E-Boats invariably turned away, straight into the Oerlikons and Browning machine gun fire of Hitchens' other section which had circled around to lie in ambush.

Lt-Commander Hitchens, who won two DSOs and three DSC's, became an enthusiastic proponent of the Holman Projector and met Treve Holman on many occasions to discuss its development. On the 'Fairmile' 'A' and 'B' boats the projector was fired by a control valve set on the bridge and upper deck and Hitchens had other refinements in mind. Early in 1943 while he and Treve Holman were dining in London, he sketched on the back of a menu card, designs for the 'Mk.4' which would be less complicated and easier to train and fire. A prototype was built at Camborne and sent up to Dover but tragically it was never to be tested. On 16 April 1943 during a fierce firefight in the early hours in the Channel, Robert Hitchens was killed by a single stray shot fired at very long range by the fleeing E-Boats.

For the rest of the war the Holman projector continued to equip merchantmen and warships. Minesweepers, 'Flower' Class corvettes, tramp steamers and even Tank landing craft disgorging 'Sherman' tanks onto the Normandy beaches all carried projectors. There were light-hearted uses when bored trawler crews used their projectors to bombard each other with potatoes, hence its nickname of the '*Potato Gun*'. Towards the end of the war the projector was further developed with the introduction of the 2 $^{1}/_{2}$ inch long-barrelled projector especially for flares. Large versions were built when the Navy found that the recoil from the throwers for their new '*Hedgehog*' AS. bombs was damaging the decks of destroyers and corvettes. Holmans produced several, including one with a 7 inch bore which used a bigger cordite propellant and was capable of firing a 55 lb. bomb over 200 yards, though both prototypes were made redundant by the end of the war. One intriguing experiment was the mounting of a long-barrelled projector on a Rolls hydraulic recoil cradle in the nose of a '*Liberator*' patrol bomber. Once a surfaced U-boat had appeared on the bomber's radar, it could be illuminated at long range by a flare from the projector and a depth charge attack launched.

Back in Camborne it was very obvious by early 1940 that it was going to be a new kind of war with the works being camouflaged, '*Fire*

Home Guards stand beside the Mk.1. 'Chough' gun, a land based short barrelled version of Holman Projector. Using a cordite charge, the 'Chough' could fire flares, mortar bombs or anti-tank rounds at quite long ranges, but did not proceed beyond the testing stage.

Watching' being organised and a strict *'Black-out'* being enforced. Once again the benches were emptied as the Territorials and R.N.R. men were mobilised, while many men volunteered without waiting for conscription. The young apprentice who had signed up in 1932, finished his time on the Sunday and joined the Royal Navy next day and on reaching Devonport barracks, was confronted by many of his mates from the foundry.

The works soon formed an L.D.V. Unit which was commanded for some time by Leonard Holman; the men parading in ordinary clothes and wearing armbands, with *'about one rifle to every twenty men'*. Things improved when the Home Guard was formed, with the company being split into two platoons of 'B' Company 9th (Cornwall) Battalion. Sentry duty and exercises were readily done after a day or night shift and the Holman Home Guard was regarded as one of the best of the Cornish units. There was the odd incident when fear of heights led one sergeant, ordinarily an excellent soldier, to refuse to climb the water tower on No.1 on a pitch-black night. *'One high spot of the platoon's history'* almost led to a court martial but was fortunately preceded by a *'famous victory'* when the garrison of Penventon was wiped out to a man.

The Camborne Works was vital in turning out components for tanks, depth charge throwers, Bailey bridges aircraft landing gear and trigger cases for Oerlikon guns and Bren gun parts. Personnel from the Royal Engineers and the RAF airfield construction units were trained on rock drills and air compressors both at the works and up at the Test Mine.

In 1942 Holmans was asked to manufacture components and produce main assembly drawings for the Polish-designed 'Polsten' 20 mm. A-A gun. The original design work for the gun was smuggled out of Poland just before

A new generation of 'Holman Girls' pose outside the works in 1942

the German invasion and its production was placed with the British Stengun Company hence its name of 'Polsten'. It was intended to be a cheaper and far less complicated gun than the Swiss Oerlikon A-A Gun.

Holmans were already making parts for Bren guns and trigger casings for Oerlikon guns but they were unenthusiastic about the Polsten, correctly believing that the contract would interfere with their ordinary war work. Half the drawing office staff had to be re-directed to work on the new jigs, tools and gauges and then twenty major components had to be re-designed.

To accommodate the Polsten production line a brand new shop, the '*N*' or '*New Factory*', with five bays and covering 65,000 square feet, was ordered by the Ministry of Supply. Holmans actually designed the new shop and supplied the builder with the gear to help erect it but there were considerable delays, although one bay was completed sufficiently quickly to serve as a lay apart store for the new equipment. Only eight machine tools were envisaged by the ministry but this soon rose to twenty-four, some of which had still not been wired up after six months, while hardening and inspection departments had to added. An additional problem was the training of '*totally unskilled women*' who had to be provided with mess rooms and general accommodation. After a very fraught year, on 29 July 1943 the first completed Polsten was given firing trials at Porthtowan. Straight away there were more major problems as welded components failed under the shock of the fast '*Blow back*' system of the gun. More dangerously, the stop-double loading mechanism was faulty and had to be totally re-designed by Holmans.

By June 1944 1000 Polsten guns had been built and within another six months No. 2000 left '*N*' shop, complete, tested and with a spare barrel, while over 120,000 gun components were turned out when the contract was cancelled that December. The Polsten was mainly intended to provide a highly portable and fast firing AA gun to support the Allied invasion of Normandy; indeed two of them were the only A-A guns dropped with the

Built for the production of the Polsten anti-aircraft gun, the 'N' Factory was used for a comparetivly short time before becoming Holman's 'PT' shop in January 1945

airborne forces at Arnhem. Many were mounted on '*Liberty*' ships or used for airfield defence while the Canadian army evolved the '*Skink*', a tank chassis boasting a quadruple A-A mounting of Polsten cannons.

Amid all this frantic activity came the death at seventy-three of Ben Cock on 1 April 1942, which ended another era as he really was the last of the rock drill pioneers who could recall the heady days of James McCulloch and the 'Cornish Rock Drill'. Despite increasing ill health he had until a few weeks before remained at work as works manager at No.1. His obituary summed up an amazing man who was '*unassuming manner, imperturbable in temperament, as courteous as he was kind hearted, well read and well grounded in the study of national and empire affairs, he understood the good parts and other difficulties of socialistic and other political affairs.*'

Sadly, he was just deprived of being at work during the royal visit when King George and Queen Elizabeth visited the works as part of the tour to Cornwall on 6 May 1942. They were met by Kenneth and Treve, who himself had been made High Sheriff of Cornwall, and it was noticed that the Queen wore on her lapel the coveted large 'H' broach exclusive to Holmans. Holman Brothers' contribution to war production was amazing, considering that it was a relatively small plant in the far west of Cornwall. The Ministry of Supply alone had 1350 air compressors and there were similar massive orders for rock drills, hoists, Rotopumps, air motors and pneumatic tools from the Admiralty and the Air Ministry. The Admiralty also had 475 depth charge throwers and 3,500 Holman projectors while the army received the 2,000 Polsten guns. Extra to all this was the production of oleo cylinders for the landing gear of '*Warwick*' and '*Wellington*' bomber and complete versions of the same for '*Spitfires*'. The machine shops also produced pins for Bailey bridges, Oerlikon gun casings, brackets for the caterpillar tracks of tanks, aircraft parts for Fairey Aviation and drop forging for the Fleet Air Arm.

Illustration: Clive Carter.

Chapter Eight

Fifty years of change

In 1945 Holman Brothers, like most of British industry, had to return to peacetime production and they appear to have adapted quicker than most, as the directors had rightly anticipated the post war boom in housing and civil engineering. There were inevitably difficulties, similar to those faced after World War One, with spares, material and manpower being in short supply while 'R and D' had ceased in 1939.

The first and biggest task came late in 1945 when 'PT', the Pneumatic tool shop, moved from the old Public rooms into the vacated Polsten gun shop. Many of the original lathes and machine tools were taken over from the Ministry of Supply and one of the first automatic lathes was installed. A bonus was the conversion of one large bay into the 'Holman Canteen', which catered not only for the expanding work force but became the centre for the social life of the company and Camborne itself. Everybody wanted to use what soon became known as the 'Holman Concert hall'. Six hundred could be seated and the small stage hosted everything from clowns, magicians and performing dogs to technical lectures and concerts by BBC "Artistes" and, of course, Camborne town Band whose director worked next door in 'PT'.

Holmans did not require exhortations by the government to 'Export or die' as, for half a century, three quarters of all they made had been foreign orders won against stiff competition. Production was soon up by 25 % and during the single month of October 1949, a record 328 drills of all types were manufactured. There were fresh orders from India, Australia and Canada; 34 'Silver Bullets' for a Turkish Copper Mine, 26 TM 60 Compressors for the South African Railways and 100 more Silver Bullets and another 26 compressors for the South Harbour Roads Board. Holman equipment was helping build the Aswan Dam and the Owen Falls Power Scheme on Lake Victoria and all these new orders were invariably published in the new company magazine.

There were also the showcase exhibitions and trade fairs, which were already pointing the way towards a European Market and the Holman Stand was prominently displayed at Milan,

Barcelona, Birmingham and many other venues. To ensure a wider audience, a company film was made in 1948. 'Serving the World' was 45 minutes long and a really comprehensive record of the work of every department. Lionel Marson of the BBC supplied the commentary.

Milton Thomas of Camborne using a drifter at the Holman Test mine, around 1952

All the directors resumed their worldwide visits to the Holman agencies or far flung mining fields. Mr Percy had one especially adventurous trip when the troubled car he had hired to take him from Cordoba to a Spanish mine, finally burned out its brakes on a mountain road and all onboard had to hurriedly disembark and shove boulders under the wheels. Mr Treve, after an arduous trip to sort out technical problems with the 'Silver Bullets' at the Aswan Dam, visited Holland and Germany before flying off to Canada to reorganise the agency. Mr Kenneth and his son Richard visited Lisbon and Barcelona while his other son James - 'Young Mr Jim' -toured every mine, bar one, in the Gold Coast Colony and returned via the agencies in North Africa.

These extraordinary trips which had been going on for years and would continue for many more, exacted a toll from among the now ageing Holman boys. Mr Leonard and his wife spent seven months travelling through Australia and New Zealand, which sapped his already frail health and he died on 1 June 1949. Lacking the fearsome energy of Treve or the great stamina of Percy, Mr Leonard was always a quiet and determined man, often self-deprecating, who despite a life spent in business and industry, found his greatest delights in the gardens and farm at 'Rosewarne'.

Treve Holman became managing director of Holmans and he decided with the others that the first ever 'Holman Week' should still go ahead in September 1949. Originally suggested as a way of creating money for charity, the 'Week' also demonstrated the Holmans strong sense of responsibility for Camborne while emphasising the role of industry in a vigorous post war Britain. Surprisingly few townspeople had been inside the foundry gates, so highly popular works tours were organised, while the 'Holman Canteen' was filled every evening. There were parades, sports and a vast fire work display. By happy coincidence 'Holman Week' also coincided with 'Camborne Shopping Week, both events giving the picture of a bustling industrial town.

1951 was a signal year for Holman Brothers Ltd. as not only did they celebrate their 150th anniversary but they also embarked upon an era of development, which slowly transformed the company into a thriving modern business. One success was the 'Dustductor' system of drilling, which was another product of the amazing mind of Treve Holman. Humidity in very deep mines prevented the use of water, so he came up with a system whereby the dust was extracted from the hole in much the same way as a vacuum cleaner and deposited well away from the working face.

Much of the 150th celebration reflected the 'fine family spirit' that had been one of their greatest strengths since the beginning. Three quarters of the employees belonged to the 'Sports Club' whose new grounds at Dolcoath Road were opened by Mr Treve, always a keen sportsman himself, on 2 May 1953 though Percy, as president of the Rugby Union, was away attending the final at Wembley.

The directors had already announced that every employee would receive an extra week's pay so the employees responded by each donating a shilling towards the cost of a special presentation made to them by the directors. This presentation was made on 29 May 1951 in the form of four anniversary dinners when, in relays of 400, the work force sat down in the canteen on four consecutive evenings, arranged according to length of service; something always jealously guarded by the 'Old hands'. Mr Treve, by now managing director, was invited by J.H. Reynolds to receive the presentation of a silver salver from William S Rodda, while Mr Percy was handed a

The presentation to the Holman Directors during the 150 year celebrations in 1951

book containing the signatures of 1,870 employees by Alfred Angove. William and Alfred were two of the oldest Holmans men but they could not rival Nicholas Curry 'Mr Nicky' who was also present. Each employee also received a copy of 'Cornish Engineers', the anniversary book written by the Bernard Hollowood, although Treve Holman himself collated and supplied most of the historical research into his company. 'Holman Week', which should have embraced a whole week of sports and entertainments including an appearance by the famous Dagenham Girl Pipers, was unfortunately washed out by the Cornish summer.

There were compensations as the 150th celebrations extended world wide to every corner of the Holman Empire. The Holman Male Voice Choir made a splendid tour of Scilly under the conductor Leonard Collins, while Holmans won a Gold medal at the Cornish Industries Fair where they displayed rock drills and the celebrated cut away model of a 'Silver Bullet'.

Beyond the celebrations it was business as usual and in June 1951 came the first of the radical changes for the company. The old office at Wesley Street had become far too cramped to cope with the rapidly expanding office staff and Mr Jim Holman, who did not wish to live at 'Rosewarne' after his father's death, offered the house as a new headquarters for the company. Some had slight misgivings about the offices being so far from the works but Rosewarne was converted and, over two weekends, everything was shifted down the road, people happily going to work despite the tales of the headless horseman who supposedly rode up the drive on winter nights.

Lack of space was also a problem at No. 1 and in August 1951 Holmans bought the old Bartle Foundry, which was largely used for maintenance work by South Crofty Mine and plans were laid for its development for lighter foundry work. The greatest prize of the whole year was revealed on 19 December 1951, when it was announced that Treve and Percy Holman had become directors of their once bitter rivals, 'Climax' Rock drill and Engineering Works. There was no longer the business to support such complementary firms in a Britain that faced 'gigantic economic problems' and Holmans were undoubtedly the more powerful of the two enterprises. 'Climax' stopped production of

Over 200 Holman rock drills, some assembled at Johannesburg, were used on the imense scheme on the Zambesi at the Kariba Gorge, and here machines are drilling the rockface that stood between the upstream entrance to the diversion tunnel and the Zambesi, shortly before it was blasted in December 1957.

pneumatic tools and gradually the two companies merged until, by 1962, they had formed the 'Holman Group' with Mr Percy Holman as chairman.
In the midst of continuing success came the sudden loss of Kenneth Holman, who, in poor health for some years, died on 31 December 1954, having been at work at 'Rosewarne' only the previous day. It was a considerable blow for the Holman family, yet they proved as resilient as ever and, despite the bleakness of the home economy, they still had their excellent foreign business. More new products were developed, like the 'Tractair', a small tractor mounted air compressor and, of course, the 'Silver Three', perhaps their most versatile and best known rock drill.

One versatile product which had been inherited from Climax was 'Maxam', whose name was created so as to read the same from both directions, but in reality was a sophisticated technology based on air pressure. Its uses were wide and various and Maxam valves and allied components controled all kinds of manufacturing process, from the food industry right through to mining operations. One of the largest Maxam valves, with a 6 inch bore, was made up in haste from spare material for the Greensplatt Cornish pumping engine which had been re-erected at a local industrial museum. Part of the production process was the bonding of the piston to the rod, using a special adhesive, which then had to be baked in considerable heat. This tempted one worker to hot up his pasty in the same oven, forgetting that his meal was in a plastic box; the pasty emerged with the crust converted to a form of plastic armour and he was left to scrape out the contents. One development from Maxam was the 'Fluid Logic control system which relied upon differential pressures created by the interruption of a constant flow of air. When the Queen Mother visited Holmans in May 1967 she unveiled the commemorative plaque by breathing across a fluid logic system which, much to her delight, caused the curtains to part.

Another successful adopted product was the Goodyear Pump, patented by James Wallace

Europa Point Light House at Gibraltar, still contains a Holman Compressor installed in the early 1960's

Goodyear. Working on the Archimedian Screw principle, the pump was a superior example of technology that required very fine production methods. Within its limits the pump, although designed for water, was capable of shifting such diverse materials as sand, chemicals and molasses. Many thousands were built until the Goodyear plant was phased out in the mid-1970s.

One innovative project was the gas turbine air compressor which was initiated after a chance conversation at the 1953 Farnborough Air Show between a Holman director and a designer from 'Power Jets' (R. & D.), a company which had been created by the government to exploit the technology generated by the development of the jet engine by Sir Frank Whittle. The potential market was the 'DEW' line, a chain of early warning radar stations to be erected across northern Canada and the goal was a compressor light enough to be airlifted into the wilds and able to stand arctic conditions. Treve Holman became involved and after further meetings, the concept designs for the T.100 turbo compressor came in February 1954.

The T.100 was largely built at Holmans with outside firms supplying the specialist jet engine components. Assembly and testing were done in the old 'Climax' stores and canteen, with the T.100 being tested in limited form in April 1958. 1,000 hours of testing and modification ensued when it was discovered the compressor could be started with a 3-speed bicycle. By July 1960 the T.100 was operational but the innovative design was cancelled. Holmans did not have the capacity to make the more advanced gas turbine parts and the fuel consumption, as had always been emphasised, was very high. Anyway, in the meantime Holmans had developed the first of the 'Rotair' range of single stage, rotary screw compressors that were to became a standard machine.

Holman Brothers Ltd had undergone the first of many changes when, in July 1957, it was announced that, with expansion and post war inflation having *'combined to put a very severe strain on our resources'*, Holmans was *'Now a Public Company'* and being quoted on the Stock Exchange. It was the beginning of a new era and the directors responded with their usual worldwide campaigns for business. 'Mr Percy' vanished behind the 'Iron Curtain' on a month's visit to Poland. Meanwhile Treve Holman, despite increasingly poor health, went *'Round the World in 35 Days'*, as the trip was headlined in the 'Holman Magazine' in the spring of 1955. He visited New York, San Francisco, Sydney, Melbourne and Calcutta, still finding time to visit the New York Botanical gardens, though he was thwarted from seeing their collection of rare magnolias, his great love. He also managed to call on the vice President of the American Newcomen Society in Pennsylvania to receive a generous donation for the Cornish Engines Preservation Society.

Considering his age and health, such a trip must have taken a far heavier toll than most realised, yet he resumed his normal hectic activities. His death, on 1 June 1959, while combining a holiday with business in Lisbon, really marked the end of the old Holman Empire, leaving Mr Percy Holman as the only survivor of the last

The West African gold mines had always been excellent customers for Holman machinery like this drifter at work in the late 1950's.

generation of Holman boys. Treve Holman's career had been remarkable, embracing a staggering variety of interests combined with what he regarded as his civic, commercial and social responsibilities, while his *'pioneering spirit and original mind'* had ensured him a place among the greats of Cornish engineering. He designed a new bathroom for 'Tregenna' as easily as his own new car in 1913 while his extraordinary energy earned him an appropriate epitaph, written for one of the Holman Concert parties during the 1930s

'When Mr Treve is on the job
the matter calls for haste
he likes the paper on the wall
Before you mix the paste'.

By the sixties, the Holman works had developed into a modern engineering works and when the author joined 'PT' in 1963, still employed over 2000. These were still the years of the *'Noonday stampede' when, as the hooter blew, hundreds of 'Grimy little men in boilersuits and big boots'* poured out of the main gate at No.1 overwhelming anything or anybody that was unwise enough to stand between them and their dinner. There was no such urgency when the hooter blew at one o'clock, and one of the most remarkable sights was that of the many 'old hands' who pedalled their bicycles so incredibly slowly that they alone seemed to have achieved a supreme balance between gravity and momentum.

P.T. never had the bleak isolation generated by the ultra modern production lines, mainly as the work itself came in what were, compared with a car plant, ridiculously small batches. There was still the atmosphere akin to that of belonging to the crew on a large ship, where dry, often riotous humour made bearable the long night shifts, or standing before a machine covered with sweat, oil and dirt and seeing nothing of the hot summer's afternoon except a glimpse of blue sky through the ventilation louvers in the roof. Nobody could resist the temptation to use the small 'Yale' trucks as high-speed scooters, occasionally with disastrous results. The door on one foreman's small office in 'P.T.' was invariably

The demolition of the old battleship 'Warspite' after she ran ashore off Prussia Cove in April 1947 became one of the epics of marine salvage. In July 1950 she was finally refloated at the second attempt, and kept afloat by a battery of Holman compressors, seen mounted next to the aircraft hanger amidships, was towed around to her berth at Marazion where much more Holman equipment was used to help break her up.

left unlatched and, with a smart wallop from a fast moving Yale could easily be flung wide open. That is until the night he chose for once to shut it, and the resultant spectacular impact left him still seated at his desk but hidden by the wrecked door. The quest for a *'bit of stick',* firewood to the uninitiated, was an obsession throughout the works and no box or packing case could survive for long, regardless of size. The author can still recall one exceptionally large and highly expensive packing crate, parked under the full glare of floodlights, that physically shrank as the nightshift progressed and that without any of the sounds of the usual surreptitious sawing. By dawn it had most certainly been reduced to kindling, chopped neatly to fit scores of *'Crouse bags'*. Some of those on nightshift would be equally tempted to snatch a quick doze, occasionally with unforeseen results. One radial driller, secreted under a pile of bags on top of a locker found himself being used as a convenient step by his foreman, who, despite being tall found it necessary to jump up and down to reach a window, and he was wearing large *'Hobby Boots'*.

There were still many 'old hands' who would regale the newcomer with stories of Holmans in the old days and there were other reminders, like copies of drawings for machines initialled by some long forgotten draughtsman back in the 1920s. Or there was the amazing horizontal milling machine, resembling a vast four poster bed that, despite coming to Holmans second hand in 1919, regularly and accurately milled the slides on the big SL.14.drifters, which one old timer remembered being sent off to the Witwatersrand in batches of 25 a week. Then there was the famous batch of drifters for Finland which were dismounted from their cradles and fitted with straight bar handles like a road ripper, which led

Holman air compressors onboard Mowlem's construction barge which moored off the Pendeen cliffs during the late summer of 1961, was used by Geevor Tin Mines in the first bid to seal the under sea breach into the workings of the old Levant mine

to endless speculation that they were going to be used by some race of Nordic giants.

The works was still expanding and by the summer of 1963, a new compressor erection shop had been built on the site left by the demolition of Centenary Row East, originally fifteen old miners' houses. A 'Queen's Award to Industry' came in 1966, followed by a visit from the Queen Mother in May the following year when she was received by Mr Jim Holman, chairman of the company. New machines were still being added, like the general purpose and very small 'Silver Feather' and the 'Silver 82', which was developed from the ubiquitous 'Silver Three'.

In 1968 the merger of Holman Bros. with their erstwhile rivals Broomwade of High Wycombe to form CompAir Holman, seemed the path to continuing success, much in the way that Holmans had taken over 'Climax' back in 1951. Another era had ended that same year when Percy Holman or 'Mr Percy' or 'Pip' retired as chairman of the Holman group after serving fifty-three years with the company. If the 'Holman boys' had been a rugby team then certainly Treve would have been the captain and Percy the prop - forward. Sadly 'Mr Percy' saw little of his well earned retirement, as he died suddenly at the age of seventy three at a County Rugby semi-final at Redruth, with Cornwall already beating East Midlands, on 6 February 1969. He had been a life-long Rugby man, having played both for Camborne and Cornwall and been President of the Rugby Union, though he was an equally enthusiastic yachtsman sailing from the Helford River. His business and civic career had been exemplary and he had received the O.B.E. in 1960. Yet 'Mr Percy' seemed to have had more robust adventures than the other 'Holman Boys', such as when, in 1933, seated in the back of a Gypsy Moth, he flew through a tremendous monsoon while his pilot tried to find a course from Karachi to Bombay.

J.F. Holman, 'Mr Jim' had already taken over as chairman of the Holman group after 'Mr Percy's' retirement, but he died in December 1974 at the comparatively young age of fifty-eight. He had spent his youth mining in Canada and after service with the RAF had taken over as the company's London director in 1950. He would undoubtedly have taken the modernisation of Holmans even farther.

Even as the Holman family slowly relinquished their command of the company formed by their great grandfather, these were still the days of the 'Foundry families' sons who had followed their fathers and grandfathers into the foundry. Some had extraordinary records of service. The Trebilcocks accumulated over 300 years of combined service but few could rival the Godolphins, who stemmed from Francis Godolphin, an ex Harvey pattern maker who joined Holmans back in 1896 and whose sons and grandsons served the Holmans for over a century.

Yet the optimism, even enthusiasm, of the seventies soon evaporated and merely became a prelude to the near destruction of heavy industry in Britain. Much of the damage had already been done and was often self-inflicted. A hankering for the old days of easy trading with a captive empire, a supine refusal to define the proper role of trade unions, the delusion of continuing superiority in foreign markets and the failure to recognise the potential of the European market, all contributed to the greatest re-shaping of British industry since the Industrial Revolution. CompAir Construction and Mining, although the world's third largest manufacturer of compressed air equipment and with a far better record than most companies, could not escape unscathed by the unforgiving economics of the 1980s.

'Rocky 2' R.B.H. Rig (Rotary Blast Hole) , delivered to Chesterhouse open cast coal site Northumberland in June 1986

In 1980 CompAir Holman was taken over by I.C. Gas at the very start of this unhappy period which had already seen the demise of Alfred Herbert Ltd, the supreme British machine tool maker, where Treve Holman had served his apprenticeship so long ago. The company's name was changed to 'CompAir', meaning that for the first time for over a century the name Holman had not been used. Other familiar names would soon be extinguished as the deepening recession struck in housing and civil engineering, seriously affecting the makers of construction plant and machinery. 'CompAir's' catalogue still offered a very wide range of products and was a publication that would have delighted the old 'Holman Boys' who, significantly, would have easily recognised the new generation of 'Silver Three's', 'P.W.'s' and 'Road Rippers', despite the innovation of noise mufflers.

An early casualty of the reorganisation was the world famous Holman Museum, which had been created in the old Public Rooms which once housed 'P.T.'. During the reorganisation after the war, Richard Gilbert had found various old drills and machines lying about the works or in the 'R. & D.' shop. He had these re-fitted with the idea they might form part of a company museum; Treve Holman's enthusiastic support was guaranteed and he suggested they also add production machines. Many other exhibits were added, most relating to Cornish mining history. Also included were the possessions of the Cornish Engine Preservation Society. The museum even appeared on the famous children's T.V. programme 'Blue Peter' and at one period attracted 6000 visitors a year. Yet by 1980 it was considered to have no role in the modern company. Perhaps it did not, but the arbitrary decision to dispose of this unique collection to a small industrial theme park effectively deprived Camborne of the opportunity to exploit its industrial heritage in years to come.

1985 was to be a year of dramatic and radical change for what remained of the Holman Empire. After years of heavy losses, Compair was at last marginally profitable but by February there were alarming rumours that the Camborne works might close and the whole operation might be transferred to Marlow; the compressor plant at Desborough having already shut down. What ensued, to use a once popular phrase, was an 'Agonising re-appraisal' of the company's entire future.

By the summer, the inconceivable was being proposed that rock drill production should cease after 105 years. Holman equipment was still being made to withstand ' enormous punishment' and be 'exceptionally reliable', a legacy of the days when Holmans proudly boasted that everything they made included 'One third for efficiency'. It took an hour and half to forge a rock drill cylinder while the Japanese made the same component from a steel pipe, producing a machine which was just as effective and also cheap enough to be discarded at the end of a contract. The days of the 'Silver Bullet' and the 'Silver Three' appeared to have ended and underlined the unpalatable truth that survival relied upon rationalisation in production, marketing and development.

The painful process began in September 1985 when I.C. Gas, who wished to concentrate on their oil and gas business, sold CompAir Holman to the Siebe Group, an acquisitive and hard edged

A Holman air compressor driving a well sinking rig in the suburbs of the Korean capital Seoul in 1973.

conglomerate with a large engineering sector. Rock drill production virtually ceased and within weeks came 500 redundancies, at a time when most large employers, including the last tin mines, were already in deep trouble. The effect was similar to that of the closure of Dolcoath Mine back in 1921 but now there was little or nothing to cushion the devastating loss of jobs and the effect this would have on the town of Camborne.

The Holman work force had been shrinking over the years from about 3000 in 1962 to 2,275 in 1974 until in 1985, only about 850 people remained at the Camborne factory. The new redundancies reduced it to 330 with a further 120 employed outside Cornwall. Production schedules and working practices were revised and a vigorous new approach to marketing and development wiped away the last vestiges of the cosy and paternal days of the old Holman empire. Even the big office block was sold off to Kerrier District Council and the 'Board Room' brought back to the main works after an absence of thirty-five years. The current Managing Director, Peter Fitch, recognised the value of the name 'Holman' and renamed the company 'CompAir Holman'.

Reminiscent of the big tunelling machines that so impressed the Cornish engineers and mine captains a century before, the 'Autopanto' was a self - propelled twin boom rig with the hydraulics worked by a vane type air motor. Seen here underground in the Test Mine in 1975, the 'Autopanto', mounted Silver 95, chain driven drifters and were capable of deep drilling in very narrow headings.

There was an increasing emphasis on the civil engineering market rather than mining, though there was still good business to be had in Sierra Leone, Nigeria and Ghana. The 'Zitair' range of air compressors was further developed and improved which soon resulted in substantial orders from plant hire companies and also from Cornwall County Council. A new departure was rough terrain dumper trucks, first displayed at the Birmingham Construction Exhibition in March 1987 while German 'Ahlman' 4 -wheel drive excavators were also built and marketed.

The works still sprawled over 22 acres and embraced buildings that would have been familiar to old John Holman, standing alongside shops like 'P.T.' dating from the war and others erected in the 1950s and 60s. Many housed plant and machinery that was either redundant or obsolescent and a radical solution was needed to accommodate a proposed new 'R & D' department and assembly hall, equipped with the latest laser and computerised technology. Essentially the Holman works as it had been known for a century would be swept away and its demise would help finance the new development by taking advantage of the then continuing boom in supermarket building.

A 303AM 'Airleg' at the test mine 1977

Many welcomed the demolition of the *'Drab Victorian buildings'* at the entrance to the town and their replacement by a glittering new supermarket, which was actually 'Tesco' moving from just the other end of Camborne, where the original Camborne School of Mines had been already flattened for the supermarket's benefit. By the winter of 1989 the whole of the frontage of Holmans, including the ornate granite office

A 303 AM, equipped with an integral steel muffler, tested alongside a 303H, with a plastic muffler, at the Holman test mine in 1975.

block and the old foundry, was steadily being pulled down. The last traces of the old railway line to Boiler Works vanished, while the re-routing of the road up to Foundry Road obliterated the old main entrance which had seen the passing of generations of Holmans men.

By the following year, CompAir Holman was being referred to as a 'modernised multi-million pound manufacturing plant' and had installed the only computer-controlled laser cutter for metal plate in the UK. The company was awarded the coveted Ministry of Defence 'AQUAP' designation and continued to expand, though there were still occasional setbacks like the effect that trouble in the Middle East had on the construction markets. New products were added and others phased out while new markets were added, such as Holman compressors providing the power to clean down North Sea oil rigs. Robotic and precision welding enabled the company to produce components in house that had previously been subcontracted and even the headquarters block was refurbished to provide an impressive new frontage.

During the last decade CompAir Holman has continued the tradition of heavy engineering in Camborne begun by Nicholas Holman two

Holman Voltrack on demonstration, circa 1975

hundred years before in the early days of the Industrial Revolution. It is a different kind of engineering from what was familiar even twenty years ago. Men and machines have been replaced by fewer men and far more advanced machines and the days of the crowded, noisy and bustling machine shop have gone for good. Their passing may be lamented by those who can afford the luxury of nostalgia but progress, regardless of casualties, is unstoppable and it is worth remembering that Richard Trevithick, the greatest Cornish engineer and fast friend of Nicholas Holman, used his extraordinary genius to improve and go forward.

Illustration: Clive Carter.

Illustration: Clive Carter.

Going up Camborne hill coming down

The final chapter in this history of the Holman engineering empire must be that of the working replica of Richard Trevithick's Road Locomotive, the 'Roaring Puffing Devil' which went up Camborne Hill on the stormy Christmas Eve of 1801. It was the culmination of four years of hard work by the Trevithick Society, who were the successors of the old Cornish Engines Preservation Society. The Trevithick Society had already brought back under steam the historic winder whose rescue, sixty years before, had inspired the first bid to preserve Cornwall's industrial heritage.

From drawing board to construction had been a formidable task as enthusiasm and dedication had to be matched by an equally vigorous campaign to raise the necessary funds. A large number of Cornish companies were recruited to the project and in 1999 an approach was made to CompAir Holman. The ensuing discussion could have been held with any of the old 'Holman Boys' . In reply to the projectors' comment that it was a pity that the company no longer had apprentices, Mr Geoff White who later became a Vice President of CompAir Holman, said, 'We still have plenty of apprentices, except that they are retired and wandering around Camborne but they are still our apprentices'.

Two centuries might have passed but Holmans still retained that glorious commodity, known in the American Space Programme as 'The Right Stuff''. The subsequent building of the replica took place in an atmosphere of curiosity and pride, though considerable skill and ingenuity was demanded to reconcile the engineering practices of 1801 to those of a modern plant. The Holman engineers working to the exacting standards of high pressure air compressors were horrified that many locomotive components required 'gaps' rather than tolerances. The greatest advantages of CompAir Holman hospitality were the ready access to machine tools, the skills and enthusiasm of all those involved and a splendid working environment. Over the coming months their unfailing encouragement and generosity was crucial and the Trevithick Society and the people of Camborne will always owe CompAir Holman a great debt of gratitude.

In March 2000 the locomotive's boiler arrived from the Deepdale Engineering Co. of Dudley, ready to be mounted on a stout oak chassis which had been precision planed by David Ball Construction of Redruth. Other components like nuts, bolts, wheels and furnace fittings, were added in the coming months, all individually and generously made by many other firms. Such was the progress that the locomotive was displayed in public for the first time on Trevithick Day in April 2000 and, being partly under steam, created an enthusiastic response from townspeople and visitors alike. A year later the 'Roaring Puffing Devil' is undergoing road trials in the yard at CompAir Holman, ready for its maiden run up Camborne Hill in April 2001, two centuries after Nicholas Holman helped realise Richard Trevithick's dreams of his 'Road locomotive' or perhaps as it should be known, the world's first motor car.

Camborne Plant 2001

Amada CNC Turret Punch

4 Metre Bender

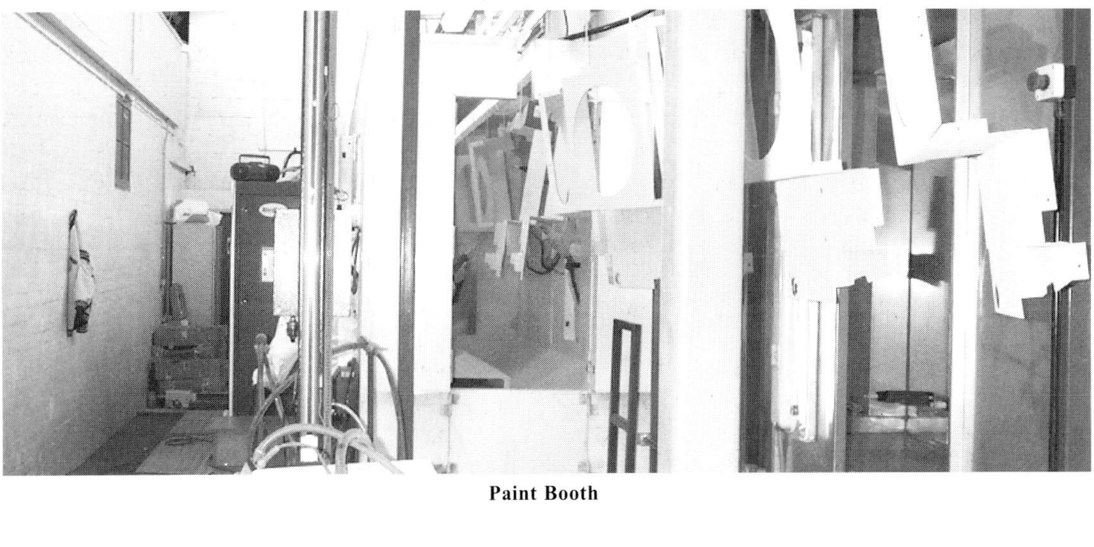

Paint Booth

FIRST AID